HAND ME A DR PEPPER, PLEASE

HAND ME A DR PEPPER, PLEASE

A *fresh* LOOK AT THE ISSUE OF CHRISTIANS AND SOCIAL DRINKING

RANDY SHULER

TATE PUBLISHING & *Enterprises*

Published by Tate Publishing & Enterprises, LLC
127 E. Trade Center Terrace | Mustang, Oklahoma 73064 USA
1.888.361.9473 | www.tatepublishing.com

Tate Publishing is committed to excellence in the publishing industry. The company reflects the philosophy established by the founders, based on Psalm 68:11,
"The Lord gave the word and great was the company of those who published it."

Book design copyright © 2010 by Tate Publishing, LLC. All rights reserved.
Cover design by Tyler Evans
Interior design by Jeff Fisher

Published in the United States of America

ISBN: 978-1-61566-590-7
1. Religion, Christian Life, Social Issues
2. Religion, Christian Life, Personal Growth
10.01.012

Acknowledgments

To Jack Cauwels and Max Barnett:

Your support for and belief in this project have been invaluable, as well as the compelling consistency of your walk with our Lord!

Thanks also to Gene, Mom, Red, Pat, and others who have been a source of encouragement and help in getting this book into the hands of others! Debbie, thank you for believing this book might help other families avoid what you have had to endure.

And most importantly, to my wife, Caryn, and children—John, Richie, Jamie, and Kristin:

You've been great sounding boards, as well as a constant inspiration to see this book through! Thank you! Your lifestyle choices are truly yours now. May this provide a more thorough understanding as to the *why* Mom and I have made the choices we've made!

Table of Contents

Foreword

I am delighted Randy Shuler has written this book. The consumption of alcohol destroys countless lives every day. The gateway to becoming addicted is often social drinking. Others indicate they drink to be able to sleep better, for stress release, for their heart, and for other reasons. Liver damage often results, so drinking alcohol for health reasons can be validly questioned.

Some say alcoholism is a disease. What an amazing deception! I cannot say to you, "I promise you that you will never have cancer." I can say, "I promise that you will never become an alcoholic, if you never take a drink of an alcoholic beverage."

The author gives some great instructions for the person who truly wants his life to be a blessing and not a hindrance to others. He has thought long and hard about the issues related to alcohol consumption.

I wish every young person would read this book with an open mind. Having given most of my life to working with university students, I have seen the devastation alcohol has caused on college and university campuses. No freshman comes to the campus planning to become an alcoholic, but seniors leave every year who are addicted and who are on the road to destroying their lives and deeply hurting their families.

In this book, you will find important information to ponder. I hope you will consider it prayerfully and make a wise choice regarding alcoholic beverages. "Do not look on the wine when it is red, when it sparkles in the cup, when it goes down smoothly; at the last it bites like a serpent, and stings like a viper" (Proverbs 23:31–32).

—Max Barnett

Director of Student Ministry (37 years),
University of Oklahoma

Professor and Consultant for
Collegiate Ministries

Author, *A Guide for Discipling Students on College Campuses*, Lifeway

Introduction

Recently, I was having a friendly conversation with a man in my office. We were talking about a wide range of topics, from personal hobbies to food to places we had both lived. He was a regular attendee at the church I pastor, and our conversation was sprinkled with a few "more serious" questions about church, theology, and the like, when he asked a question that I've been asked literally dozens of times. The circumstances surrounding *the* question are always different, but *the* question remains the same.

Andy (my friend) told me a story where he had attended a wedding reception in which he found himself sitting next to a pastor. The pastor was from a mainline denominational church yet different from ours. The kind reverend got up to get something to drink and asked Andy if he could get him something too. It was a kind gesture, and Andy requested a soda or water.

"After he returned to the table," Andy told me, "the pastor proceeded to slam three glasses of scotch on the rocks. It blew me away!" Then he asked, "Can he do that?"

Well, my mind was a blur with potential answers: "Of course, he can; he just did," "That's what they do in that denomination," or, "He could, but we can't. You see, we're a little old fashioned. That's what we do in our denomination."

Over several years, I have been asked *the* question, and I have learned that pithy responses do not provide an adequate answer. In fact, they often add more confusion than solutions to the issue. And what's more, it's really not a denominational issue. Those who do and those who don't drink socially are spread across varied denominations. Contrary to what some might think, there really are no formally fixed standards in our particular denomination.

I proceeded to tell my friend that *the* question of whether or not a Christian should drink or abstain from alcohol is better handled by taking the time to seriously think it through, rather than to simply come up with a quick answer. To truly answer the question of social drinking, we must develop a set of principles that will provide guidance for our own faith experience as well as understanding of the choices other people make on their spiritual journey.

Connected to this question is a host of sister questions, such as: Is it wrong for Christians to participate in social drinking? Is it right? Does having a glass of wine with your meal constitute a sin? Didn't Jesus drink wine? Does the Bible prohibit drinking or being drunk? Aren't teetotalers just old fashioned? Where does legalism fit into the picture? And don't I have liberty to drink alcohol, as long as it's in moderation?

These are just a few of the many challenges that stem from the issue of Christians and social drinking.

As our culture continues to grow in its pursuit, advertisement, and promotion of alcoholic beverages, I'm finding widespread confusion and even conflicting messages being communicated within the Christian community. In fact, that's why I began thinking a book might be helpful. It seems as if the topic of Christians and alcohol is on a lot more minds that most would ever guess. (I can honestly say the questions I have entertained have not come about as a result of my prompting. A person can lose friends really fast if he chooses to use this topic as a short sermon on the evils of our age. I've discovered that I gain listening ears when I merely explain why I don't drink after a person, usually over time, begins to wonder why I seem to abstain from alcohol.)

This book is an attempt to take a sincere look at a significant issue once largely regarded taboo in the Christian community but increasingly accepted among Christians in today's culture.

The purpose is to help Christians develop a God-honoring-lifestyle practice regarding the usage of alcohol. My desire isn't to condemn those who drink socially, but it is my desire to provide a compelling argument well founded in Scripture to reconsider. May it be noted that the focus is on integrating biblical principals and truths within the context of our North American culture. This is key to our understanding. Alcohol consumption in the first century had some similarities to our day and age, yet there were also grave differences. These differences, although not our principal concern, must, in the least, be acknowledged.

Therefore, the primary application for this study is for Christ-followers in the North American culture.

Whether you are a social drinker, have an occasional glass of wine, or abstain from all alcohol, I ask that you read this book through to the end. You may or may not agree with every reason I don't drink, but I think we owe it to ourselves, our children, our brothers and sisters in the faith, and even our culture to give serious thought to a lifestyle practice that may have greater implications than a lot of people realize.

For many, the issue of social drinking may be such a small issue that they intentionally give little or no thought to whether they drink or don't drink. It's just not a big deal to them. Yes, there may be weightier issues in life, and I'm sure there is an abundance of books to cover those big problems; but do not confuse smallness with a lack of significance. Just because an issue is considered small does not mean it is insignificant. To any person who has had to deal with termites, it is clear that something doesn't have to be big to cause considerable damage!

I am a pastor of a church, and I am in the unenviable position to have to deal with the damage, the fallout caused by alcohol. From addiction to divorce, to crime to accidental death and injury, alcohol is all too often a significant factor in broken bodies, broken lives, and broken homes.

On the one hand, I'm grateful that God has allowed me, as well as many others, to help people who have discovered the dark side of alcohol use and abuse. On the other hand, I feel in our culture the Christian community is polarizing itself on this issue. On the one side are the teetotalers who do little more than dangerously lob rules and clichés at anyone who differs. While on the other side, there seems to be little concern or thought given to a lifestyle practice once considered out of bounds among Christians. Is it possible to keep one eye open to the abuse of alcohol while closing the other eye to the widespread use of alcohol? In other words, is there not a correlation in our culture between use and abuse? Either way, I find many people on both sides of the issue who really haven't given serious thought as to whether they do or don't, should or shouldn't drink socially! That's all I'm asking: Will you give serious thought to the issue of social drinking? Will you think it through?

The Goal

Building a Foundation of Principles, Not Simply Establishing a Set of Rules

The issue of social drinking was much easier when I was a child. "We don't drink," was my parents' answer to queries about the absence of alcohol in our home. When asked, "Why not?" they often responded, "Because God doesn't want us to." As I grew older, that answer no longer seemed to be sufficient. The problem is that this issue is not self-evident. "Thou shall not murder" or "Do not steal" are self-evident commands. That means within our culture, it is still blatantly obvious *why* a person should refrain from murder and thievery. Even cultures that pay little attention to Judeo-Christian values view these behaviors as destructive to civilization and simply wrong. These are "universal sins."

But other practices and behaviors are not as self-evident. What kind of music a person listens to, the manner and style of dress, and the books one reads or movies one watches are not as self-evident. There are no simple, matter-of-fact rules guiding these practices, that one can say, "God says, 'Thou shall not … !'" Does that mean we have the liberty to do as we please in these areas, since there is no direct command from God? Hardly. God's Word teaches us by direct, explicit commands, and it also guides us implicitly by revealing the wisdom and understanding of God's heart and mind.

What I'm after are not mere rules: "Thou shalt not drink beer!" "Thou shalt not drink any beverage if it is fermented!" Although simpler, the issue is larger in both context and purpose than simple rules. Rather, the goal is the development of principles to live by—principles that are scriptural, God-honoring, and believe it or not, intellectually sensible. I firmly believe God's commands and expectations are given to us with reason and purpose in mind. When we begin to think with his mind, then his commands not only become our principles to live out, but they make sense!

In approaching the subject of alcohol, there are two guiding thoughts, which we must build together in a balanced way in order to form a foundational principle. Picture in your mind a seesaw, where on one end is "Christian freedom" and on the other, there's the command to "not cause a brother or sister in the faith to stumble."

Paul spells out both in 1 Corinthians. The guidance of,

But food does not bring us near to God; we are no worse if we do not eat, and no better if we do.

1 Corinthians 8:8 (NIV)

must be balanced by the truth of verse nine,

Be careful, however, that the exercise of your freedom does not become a stumbling block to the weak.

1 Corinthians 8:9 (NIV)

In verse eight, Paul is reminding us that it's not the exterior but the interior that makes a difference to God. Issues of the heart are where important matters like being right with God are located. The context of 1 Corinthians 8 is the issue of whether or not a Christian should eat meat (food) that had been offered to pagan idols. The Jewish laws prohibited it. The early Jewish Christians also viewed it as a prohibition. However, the Gentile believers (a different cultural background) saw nothing wrong with it. To them, it was just a piece of meat.

Paul is saying food (and presumably drink)—although not insignificant—are relatively minor in comparison to faith, love, and submission of the heart to the Lordship of Christ.

We can cite far too many instances similar to the religious tithers of the New Testament, where people have overlooked issues of the heart while keeping the externals of God's law. Jesus told the religious leaders that they had ignored the "important things of the law: justice, mercy, and faith," even though they had given a tenth of their spices. In the same passage, Jesus went on to say, "You should tithe, yes, but you should not leave undone the more important things" (Matthew 23:23 NLT).

That being said, Paul also warns us that our freedom can become a stumbling block to others. We must be cautious not to abuse our freedom in Christ. Abuse happens when our freedom causes another to stumble in their faith or when we convey a mixed message. The mature (or maturing) Christian, not the weaker (less mature) person, is accountable for actions that could produce a potential barrier to another person's faith journey.

The two thoughts are visited again in Galatians:

It is for freedom that Christ has set us free. Stand firm, then, and do not let yourselves be burdened again by a yoke of slavery.

Galatians 5:1 (NIV)

balanced with,

You, my brothers, were called to be free. But do not use your freedom to indulge the sinful nature; rather, serve one another in love.

Galatians 5:13 (NIV)

Here Paul warns that we must not return to legalism! Paul had firsthand experience in being set free from legalistic religion. He had studied under one of the great rabbis of modern Judaism, Gamaliel. Paul had become a Pharisee and was passionately zealous for keeping the law. Yet the chains of legalism stifled his spiritual quest to know and please God, until that day on the road to Damascus and his all-important, life-changing encounter with the living Christ. From then to his death, he would raise the banner of liberty in Christ.

Once again, however, he warns us not to allow freedom to feed a sinful nature! The sin nature is so powerful and prevalent in each of us that we must be intentional about keeping it in check. Paul reminds us in Romans 6 that we have died to sin and have no reason to live in it any longer. In essence we are to die to and even bury the old sin nature so as to leave it behind. Followers of Christ have been set free from sin's power and abiding presence, because their sin nature dies to sin the moment we are "immersed in" Christ. This is a statement of truth or theological fact; however, the very need for a reminder tells us that our tendency is to dig up the old "dead" body (sin nature) and drag it around. Sometimes, in an effort to return to the old nature, it seems we're intent on giving CPR to something that will only bring back sin, guilt, and even pain into our lives. How many times have we asked ourselves, Why did I do that? And then out of frustration over doing that, which we know will only bring heartache, we wonder if we're too weak to be a Christ-follower. The answer? We must learn to live a "crucified life" daily. That means we must die to self daily, sometimes hourly.

If we're not careful, our freedom can indulge a nature that is supposed to be dead and buried. It is a nature easily deceived and given to sin. In the end, our freedom can open the door to the bondage of an old sinful nature, choking the very life out of those claiming to be free. Nowhere is this better understood and observed than in the culture that promotes social drinking.

The point taken from Paul's admonition to live in freedom without indulging the sin nature or causing others to stumble is simply this:

> *Rather than establish rules not to break, our goal should be to build a set of "Lifestyle Principles" to live by.*

If put together properly, these principles should answer the question, What would Jesus do in our culture regarding social drinking? and then help us live up to his example. The answer isn't a hard and fast rule that if broken condemns a person; rather you will discover a set of emerging principles that if followed will lead to a more victorious, fruitful, and God-honoring lifestyle.

We must not overlook the fact that drunkenness is taboo. We will not argue the issue of drunkenness, since the Bible is extremely clear about the subject and the experiences of the world teach us the same lessons. In other words, it is self-evident: "Do not get drunk on wine, which leads to debauchery!" (Ephesians 5:18 NIV).

The issues of social drinking are not as simplistic. People often ask me whether I drink, meaning of course if I drink alcoholic beverages. "No," I will reply, "but I would have a Dr Pepper." Over the years several passages and principles from Scripture began to materialize that would time and again affirm this decision *not* to drink alcohol. As more people began to ask me where in Scripture do I find such a lifestyle principle, I discovered not one or two but many reasons along with many passages of Scripture that led me to practice a lifestyle of abstention from alcohol.

What follows is a list of ten reasons I do not include alcohol in my lifestyle. Any one reason alone might not be enough to completely convince a person. But as reason stacks upon reason, I believe a clear picture will emerge that reveals the Bible is not foggy on the issue of drinking. The issue is more black and white than many think.

I encourage you to read all ten reasons. Consider each one separately. Then see them as a whole. If you begin to discover the bigger picture is truly an accurate depiction of the sum of the parts, then a principle has emerged that you must either follow or ignore. Our challenge in this world is to always follow where God's truth leads no matter what pop culture says. May God's grace and Spirit of truth guide you as you consider the ten reasons why my lifestyle doesn't include social drinking.

Appearances

REASON #1:

I Don't Drink Because I Want to Abstain from the Appearance of Evil

Abstain from all appearance [every form] of evil.

1 Thessalonians 5:22 KJV

Do not get drunk on wine, which leads to debauchery. Instead, be filled with the Spirit.

Ephesians 5:18 NIV

Whether or not drinking *appears* to be evil can be debated. On the one hand, it can be argued that wine or alcohol is never labeled as *sin*. However, on the other hand, since drunkenness is sin, would it stand to reason that anything connected to drunkenness could give the appearance of evil?

Let me pose this scenario: What if a nationally known and highly respected Christian leader or evangelist was involved in an auto accident and the driver of the other car was seriously injured? What if the authorities discovered an open bottle of wine (or a partially drunk six-pack of beer) in the evangelist's car? Would it raise questions? Would it raise suspicions of drinking and driving? Would it raise suspicions of drunkenness?

What if the authorities could not conclude that the evangelist was drunk or even if he had been drinking; would that satisfy suspicions? Let's be honest, probably not. People would still wonder if the evangelist had been drinking and subsequently driving with impaired senses. People would wonder if the officers were sympathetic to the evangelist, knowing that any hint of drinking and driving would be a public relations nightmare. Would this story make headlines in the papers across our nation? Without a doubt!

You see, in this situation, it is the *appearance* of evil or wrongdoing that raises questions about the leader's character and moral choices. Judgments, whether right or wrong, good or bad, will likely be made by both believers as well as those outside of the community of faith. That's what appearances do. It would *appear* the Christian leader had been drinking whether or not he actually had been. It would be rumored that the famous evangelist or preacher was driving drunk, whether or not he had been impaired by alcohol.

Certainly, there must be high-profile Christians and Christian leaders who drink alcohol socially without fear of the *appearance of evil* stigma. Nonetheless, in our culture, within both Christian and non-Christian circles, high-profile and conservative evangelicals would likely be victimized, scrutinized, and possibly demonized by the *appearance of evil* accusation of drunkenness. If they were to be seen holding a Bud Light, especially prior to an auto accident, the media would have a field day! Can't you see the newscasts and newspapers across our country showing pictures of the evangelist at the crusade, preaching, then later that night, standing at a bar with a beer in his hand? There's just something strangely confusing about the thought of one of our nation's prominent evangelical leaders ordering a "cold one" after an exhausting evening of preaching. The words *belly-up-to-the-bar* don't seem to flow easily following an invitation to *bow your head and pray.* Would it be the same if it were a glass of red wine at a nice restaurant? Maybe. Maybe not. That would depend on whose eyes were doing the seeing. Appearance of evil is connected directly to perception.

Now for the more pertinent question: Is it any different for low-profile Christians? There shouldn't be a difference. We may be watched by fewer eyes than the nationally known leaders and evangelists, who lead worldwide ministries. But we're still being watched, and that produces a wide variety of things that could (*could,* mind you) *appear to be evil.*

This argument, as I said, can be debated. The fact is, however, if you don't drink, there's no argument, because you take away *any* thought of the appearance of evil regarding excessive alcohol consumption. In other words, it's difficult to be accused of being drunk if you cannot be accused of drinking.

Some will fight this conclusion, simply because they refuse to accept that it's up to them to remove a hindrance or stigma, even if it's a misperception. Some will say, "If people want to erroneously accuse me of the appearance of possible drunkenness simply because I have a glass of wine with my meal, it's their problem, not mine." Their reasoning may sound logical, but it's not biblical. Paul is clearly saying that it is the responsibility of the Christian to *abstain* from every form or appearance of evil. Commentator Adam Clark writes this of 1 Thessalonians 5:22:

> Do not drive your morality so near the bounds of evil as to lead even weak persons to believe that ye actually touch, taste, or handle it. Let not the form of it, "*eidov*," appear with or among you, much less the substance. Ye are called to holiness; be ye holy, for God is holy.[1]

Having said this, let me add that there may be times that the drink may *not* have the appearance of evil. On a mission trip to Romania, I was asked by a deeply devoted Romanian brother in the faith if I would drink a champagne toast with his unbelieving mother-in-law. After spending a week with her daughter and son-in-law's family, "Momma" (a nonbeliever) wanted to toast us. It was her way of saying she appreciated us. My Romanian brother, knowing that we might be teetotalers, told us if it were to make us feel uncomfortable, they would understand.

I thought briefly and asked, "Would this in any way put a stumbling block in the way of your mother-in-law to potentially receive Christ?"

"No," he said, "but it would honor her if we did."

"Would it appear to be sinful, or would it be spiritually detrimental to your children who, by the way, are watching with great anticipation?"

"Not at all," my brother in the faith replied. For a variety of reasons, in Romania, wine and champagne are common household drinks and would be seen as nothing more.

We did indeed toast the mother-in-law and felt nothing wrong about it. Now understand this point:

The appearance of evil isn't in the glass. It's in the perception of moral values of individuals within their specific culture.

So with a clear conscience we toasted. It wasn't until the twelfth or thirteenth toast that we decided our liberty had gone a little far! (Not really, I jest. We had one small toast!)

Does this mean that if I move to Romania, God won't care if I drink? Not necessarily. There are still other reasons it might not be the best choice. The Romanian toast was an exception. Remember, we're not building a system of legalistic rules. We're building a platform of principles. A platform of principles will leave room for exceptional situations.

By the way, it has been my experience in Africa, as well as South America, that drinking alcohol in any form is often considered taboo among local Christians. I remember standing around a campfire in a remote village of Zambia when a young man in his early twenties asked this question: "How should I, a committed Christian, relate to my friend who claims to be a Christian yet drinks alcohol as a consistent part of his lifestyle?" I remember telling him that the same issues face Christians in America, especially regarding the use and abuse of alcohol. Opposing lifestyle choices can certainly place Christians in a quandary with each other. We'll take a closer look at the answer to my Zambian brother's question later, but for now, the point is clear: If we look to the Europeans as positive examples with their relaxed tolerance of alcohol, let us be careful. The European society, as a whole, is far from being spiritually alert to the power and presence of God.

In regards to abstaining from the appearance of evil, some will ask, "Does this mean that I can drink as long as it's in private and not open to the scrutiny of others, who might see it as an appearance of evil?" This is a fair question, and one that I've heard highly regarded, national Christian leaders teach as acceptable. In fact, at a conference in California, I listened as a prevalent author, pastor, and Bible teacher taught that some behaviors are not biblically wrong, but we would do well to practice them only in private. While there may be some merit to his statement, I fear that this kind of thinking can become a double-edged sword bordering on a baptized version of moral relativism.

In developing principles to live by, I have discovered that it is far better for me not to have two sets of principles to live by: one for public life and one for private life. A key aspect in the application of any principle in life is the goal of consistency. At all times, in all places, can this principle be consistent in application? For what purpose would I choose to drink in secret while holding to a principle that shuns drinking in public? To me, alcohol is not that imperative!

The first reason I don't drink is to abstain from the appearance of evil. I do not want to do anything that would lead others to think the wrong thing. While it is true that I can't live my life based on what others *might* think of me, I still want to avoid things that may indeed create misleading perceptions. This is even more critical when I know in advance that a particular behavior will likely lead to a misperception.

Some might argue, "Didn't Jesus do this when he ate and drank with tax collectors and sinners? Didn't he know that it would lead to an erroneous perception that he was a glutton and a drunkard?" I will deal more specifically with this in chapters five and eight, but for now, let me reframe the question. The question isn't whether or not Jesus attended the parties of tax collectors and sinners but rather what was his behavior *at* the party? That would be a more pertinent question for us. As for the Jewish religious leaders of the first century, was their misperception of Jesus (that he was a glutton and a drunkard) born out of the idea that he was drinking alcohol or associating with alcoholics? Remember, they too used alcohol as an acceptable drink. Were not the religious leaders really upset at Jesus because he, a God-anointed rabbi or prophet, actually gave time and attention to the riffraff? Wasn't he aware of their oral traditions that restricted (quite legalistically) their association with the "unclean?"

Jesus clarified his behavior (and their motives) when he responded that it was the sick who need a doctor, implying that a doctor must give hands-on time and attention to the sick. It was obvious the sick were no longer on the spiritual radar screen of the religious leaders. They avoided the "unclean" like a plague. Their relentless focus on their own personal piety and advancement had little compassion for those who were struggling in life. The strongest rebukes of Jesus were reserved for the pseudo-religious who had refused to reach out to help the least, the littlest, and the lost.

At this point, we must be careful not to toss out the appearance issue on the basis that we, like Jesus, could be falsely accused and misunderstood. Just because Jesus ate and drank with the irreligious does not mean that we've been given license to almost any questionable behavior, as long as we can associate it with a Jesus story where he was wrongly criticized by the self-righteous! Remember, Jesus was accused of being crazy and even demon-possessed. Taken to the extreme, there are some modern-day fanatics whose behavior (especially in the pulpit or on stage) borders on lunacy. They justify their behavior on an absurd rationale that they are being wrongly accused and misunderstood just like Jesus was. We must not *stretch* the Scriptures to fit our wanton behavior.

If we believe that the Spirit of God inspired Paul to write the words in 1 Thessalonians 5:22 and if Jesus is the Son of God who lived a perfect life, then we must understand Jesus's lifestyle stayed well within the boundaries of abstaining from all appearance of evil. While it is unadvisable to live life based on what others might think and place every decision under the microscope of the public eye (especially the scrutiny of religious legalists), Paul's words to believers are, nonetheless, applicable today. We must consider and be open to recognizing lifestyle choices that could send the wrong message. This would apply to many areas of life, not just what beverage we order. For that reason (and a few others), I choose to not include drinking alcohol in my lifestyle. I do not want to do anything, especially as a lifestyle, that would lead others to think the wrong thing!

A Potential Problem

REASON # 2:

I Do Not Drink Because I Want to Prevent a Potential Problem from Starting

Who has woe? Who has sorrow? Who has strife? Who has complaints? Who has needless bruises? Who has bloodshot eyes? Those who linger over wine, who go to sample bowls of mixed wine. Do not gaze at wine when it is red, when it sparkles in the cup, when it goes down smoothly! In the end it bites like a snake and poisons like a viper.

Proverbs 23:29–32 (NIV)

This passage forbids even looking at a glass of wine with a desire to drink. It also prohibits wine tasting, as sometimes promoted at various vineyards. The wisest man in the history of the world tells us that alcohol can be poisonous and deadly, so don't even look at it, let alone drink it.

For some people, alcohol is very addicting. Studies

and professional opinions alike claim certain people have a genetic affinity toward alcoholism. "Many scientific studies, including research conducted among twins and children of alcoholics, have shown that genetic factors influence alcoholism."[2] According to research funded by the National Institute On Alcohol Abuse And Alcoholism (NIAAA), factors putting people at risk of developing alcoholism basically fall into two groups: "About half of the risk is genetic; the other half stems from environmental factors."[3] Research reports that, "50 to 60 percent of the risk for alcoholism is genetically determined."[4] In fact, children of alcoholics are about four times more likely than the general population to develop alcohol problems.[5] In one of the largest studies of its kind, The Collaborative Study on the Genetics of Alcoholism (COGA), which involved over 2200 families and about 15,000 people, revealed there are "Regions on several chromosomes that appear to contain genes affecting the risk of alcoholism."[6] COGA provided substantial evidence of a genetic link to the risk of or vulnerability to alcoholism.

You can't know if you're one of those persons until you drink. At that point it could be too late. Alcohol can become such a powerful problem that one must ask, "Is the risk really worth it?"

I know, one drink won't turn a person into an alcoholic. However, I've talked with far too many alcoholics who said, "I never intended for alcohol to become a problem." They didn't want to be an addict. However to a person, it started with the first drink. In other words, one eventually led to another, then another, then a few others, then others, until they were out of control in this area.

I know what people claim: "I can handle it," and "I'm not like that." Maybe they can, and many do prevent alcohol from becoming a real problem by their own self-control. But again, I've observed scores of others who said the same thing and found themselves in a real mess. So what does this mean to the Christian? It means that, even if you are capable of moderation and you're not predispositioned to alcoholism, can you be sure that those whom you influence—your family and friends—are also free from such genetic affinity? We must think this through!

Regarding those we love most, our family, there is another aspect of the genetic affinity toward alcohol dependency. Did you know that sometimes the addiction gene(s) may be recessive in one or both parents but dominant in one of their children? Many who struggle with alcohol addiction have discovered that a family member a few limbs up the family tree had a similar addiction. A friend of mine, who is a recovering alcoholic, discovered that alcohol addiction was found in distant relatives on both sides of the family tree even though his parents were teetotalers. Parents who drink in moderation run the risk of blindsiding one of their children, if the genetic makeup of their child is such that they have an almost inexorable inclination toward addiction.

Yes, the parents may be able to moderate their drink, but their children, if a genetic affinity has been quietly passed down, may have a very difficult time with alcohol. One teenage girl describes her first drink this way, "From the moment I drank the very first drink, my body seemed to crave more."

Something I've observed over several years is that it's impossible to stereotype the kind of individual that might become an alcoholic. Certainly, there are psychological and heredity profiles that a trained counselor or doctor might recognize, but to the general public, alcoholics can be found in every facet of life. The landscape of alcoholism spreads well beyond the typical high school/college binge drinker. They're aging women, highly organized businessmen, energetic coaches, and nutritionally minded, stay-at-home moms, who each started with an occasional drink.

At the onset of addiction, they will live in denial. They tell themselves that they can stop at any time. They fail to recognize that their choice is becoming a need. They tell those closest to them (usually a spouse) that they don't have a problem. Denial turns into a prolonged testing stage where the person may deprive himself of the drink for a few days, maybe even weeks, or sometimes months, but the thought of the next drink is never far from the forefront of their thinking. The choice that became a need has now turned into a demand. The "-ism" of alcohol is starting to take root. Alcohol is becoming, as Bill Wilson (founder of Alcoholics Anonymous) termed it, the "rapacious creditor."

Eventually, the person gives in to a secret fear that they cannot run from their need. So they take another drink, and the hole gets deeper and darker. And life becomes more difficult. Their lives and their livers are being eaten by an inability to change their addicted ways. If they continue drinking, it will likely lead to an inability to cope with problems. From there, life will take many different turns, most of which involve pain and suffering. Individuals, as well as family members, will end up bearing the scars of emotional, financial, relational, and sometimes even physical pain.

If we accept Solomon as the writer of Proverbs 23, then the wisest man in the world came to the conclusion that wine (alcohol) was dangerous, should be avoided, and not merely moderated!

One sure way to prevent a potential problem is simply don't give it an opportunity to start.

But what if you've already discovered that you can, in fact, moderate it? You can have a glass of chardonnay with dinner and feel no addictive tendencies whatsoever. Indeed, there are many who have and do drink with careful moderation. Yet there are others who weaken under extreme stress or pain, and the result will be a quiet, sometimes hidden dependence upon the power of the bottle to help them cope. I've observed this *tendency for dependency* growing stronger with age; however, alcohol dependency crosses all age groups.

Several years ago, an elderly but physically active neighbor of mine, who was also a long-standing member of our church, seemed to be captive within her home after about six or seven o'clock every evening. Months went by before I realized there might be a problem behind the unusual behavior of seldom seeing her outside of her home after a certain hour each night. Then one evening, she chanced being outside, and as we talked, I could tell from her breath she had been drinking. This was affirmed on a few more occasions. I began to realize that whenever I would knock on her door during the day, she was quick to answer; but in the evening, after that certain time, she was slow in coming to the door. She would speak through the door that she was coming, but it would always take longer than normal. And it wasn't because she was ready for bed and needing to find a robe or change clothes. One particular evening, after being invited into her home, I noticed a couple of used wine glasses in the sink, and I began to put the pieces together that her alcohol consumption was very consistent. So consistent was her behavior that I feared she had a drinking problem.

Most likely she didn't get crazy drunk every night, just a few glasses to help put her to sleep. Yet so consistent was this behavior, that in a very real sense, she was addicted. In other words, she had become dependent on a drug to help her relax enough to go to sleep. Since she didn't want anyone to know, she was being held as a captive in her own home, and the slave master was the bottle being doled out in a few unassuming glasses of wine about the same time every evening.

At this point, you may think I'm being extreme or hypersensitive. You might ask what's the problem with a little old lady using a little nightcap to help her sleep? If this were an occasional pattern of behavior, I'm not sure that there is anything wrong with it. However, it was obvious that this was more than an occasional sip of wine.

Here's the problem as I observed my neighbor. This nice lady withdrew from healthy social contact after a certain hour in the day. She couldn't go to a symphony or movie, she couldn't attend church or go to a Bible study, and she couldn't enjoy a simple evening of being with her closest friends after a relatively early hour of the evening. And I've seen the same scenario played out again and again. Similar to Cinderella running from the ball because the chariot will turn back into a pumpkin at midnight, people who are addicted to alcohol are quick to exit social settings because they know it's time to turn life over to the drink.

I had a conversation with some friends about celebrating the Christmas holidays and being with family. They laughed about their eighty-year-old grandma who had a drinking problem. Her drinking of seven or eight beers every evening kept the family on edge. They felt as though she probably had an addiction and that they needed to do something to help her, but she was 80-plus years old and likely to never stop.

Or I could tell of a seventy-eight-year-old deacon and leader in a conservative, evangelical church who had had a secret drinking problem for years. No one knew. He was a classic closet-alcoholic. After attending an AA meeting one evening, he confided to a younger Christian brother that he had a problem. He said that he had wanted to stop drinking for years but was unable. The younger man became the older man's sponsor and discovered that his elder would go to great lengths to stash his booze. The seventy-eight-year-old man would hide a fifth of whiskey in the ceiling tiles of his room at the nursing home where he lived. Not only was the alcohol a problem, but climbing up on a chair to retrieve his hidden addiction was dangerous!

Many of these elderly, hidden alcoholics cannot go to sleep without their little helper.

Or I could speak of the middle-age mother of three who would regularly attend social functions, including her children's school activities, but not after a certain hour of the evening. Nor would you see her attend a ladies' conference or even a marriage seminar if it required social interaction after sunset. There were always legitimate reasons given, but the reality was a person who had become addicted to the self-medication of alcohol.

I could also point to a young woman in her early twenties. Single, bright, energetic, great job, and by all practical purposes she had the world by the tail, yet she was a mess in her inner self. Enslavement to alcohol was creating havoc in her unseen personal life.

I could add the story of a young father who simply sat in a chair at home almost every evening drinking a few beers until he dozed off to sleep. Many people might not consider this a big deal, but his wife did. He was held captive by an addiction to alcohol, and although he held a consistent job, loved his family and life, he was not there to help his kids with homework or tuck them into bed or be the kind of husband his wife needed.

What I'm saying is that there are many people who don't resemble the stereotypical alcoholic, but alcohol holds them captive, nonetheless, with as much dependency and addiction as the boozer who sits every night at the local bar drinking until the joint shuts down.

I find it interesting that the medical community has discovered that there are a few health benefits in red wine, yet they consistently maintain that nondrinkers should *not* start drinking to gain whatever health benefit might be found. The American Heart Association cautions people to "not to start drinking ... if they do not already drink alcohol."[7] The Mayo Clinic offers this statement: "Few medical experts, if any, advise nondrinkers to start drinking."[8] Why? The benefit is not worth the risk! The potential problems associated with alcohol must have been evident to Solomon when he wrote Proverbs 23. So obvious were these potential problems that Solomon also wrote: "Wine produces mockers; liquor leads to brawls. Whoever is led astray by drink cannot be wise" (Proverbs 20:1 NLT).

How do you prevent a potential problem? Don't start!

The Stumbling Block

REASON # 3:

I Do Not Drink Because I Do Not Want to Become a Stumbling Block to Other Christians

Be careful, however, that the exercise of your freedom does not become a stumbling block to the weak.

1 Corinthians 8:9 (NIV)

It is better not to eat meat or drink wine or to do anything else that will cause your brother to fall.

Romans 14:21 (NIV)

We put no stumbling block in anyone's path, so that our ministry will not be discredited.

2 Corinthians 6:3 (NIV)

This is similar to the first reason, but it goes a bit further. Not all Christians will stumble, but some will; and we're *commanded* not to do things that might become a stumbling block.

In both 1 Corinthians and Romans, Paul was referring to his practice of not eating meat with those who thought eating it was a sin. He abstained from certain meat simply because he didn't want to place a stumbling block in the path of another believer. The meat that some believers refused to eat was meat that had been offered to idols in the pagan temples. It was not uncommon for meat offered to idols to later be sold to the local butcher. The public wouldn't necessarily know which pieces of meat had been a part of idol worship and which had not. Therefore, the unknown nature of the meat and the terrifying thought that a believer would partake of it or grant economic gain to those who did observe such detestable pagan practices caused many to simply say no to meat if they were unsure of its origin. Sometimes they would refuse to eat meat even when invited as a guest to a new friend's home (which put a real strain on small group fellowship).

Paul was clear that the meat was fine to eat. He writes in Romans 14:14: "I know and am perfectly sure on the authority of the Lord Jesus that no food, in and of itself, is wrong to eat" (NLT). God made the meat; therefore, it wasn't evil, even if it had been offered as a sacrifice in a pagan religious ceremony. Paul reasons that since pagan gods are in truth not really gods, that the only true god is the God of the Bible, and that all things (including the meat some will not eat) have been created by one Lord, Jesus Christ, then the meat in and of itself is okay to eat (see 1 Corinthians 8:4–6). And yet, Paul decided *not* to eat it because he didn't want his brother in the faith to stumble.

> Therefore, if what I eat causes my brother to fall into sin, I will never eat meat again, so that I will not cause him to fall.
>
> 1 Corinthians 8:13 (NIV)

The point is obvious. I don't drink because I don't want to cause another believer to stumble in his faith journey. So the Christian thinks, *What if I drink only with those who don't think having a glass of wine is wrong?* In other words, they only drink with other Christians who have the liberty to drink.

I ask, "Can you guarantee that every believer you drink with has a clear heart and conscience?" Remember, it's difficult to see what's going on in their heart. God may be dealing with them in ways you're unaware of. Alcohol abuse may have been a part of an old lifestyle that God delivered them from when they came to him. To that person, when "all things became new" (2 Corinthians 5:17 NIV), all things, including social habits, became new.

Or what if you're having dinner with a person who has alcoholism in their family and God has been speaking to their conscience about abstaining from alcohol for the sake of a family member who has just found sobriety. You may be unaware of their situation, so you order a glass of wine with your meal and unknowingly throw them back into a personal quandary. They are now tempted to ignore their conscience, thinking they must be hypersensitive or old fashioned. The end result is that they may violate their conscience and possibly God's leading, making it doubly tough on the recovering family member. This "turning a deaf ear" to the Spirit's leading has yet another negative consequence; it causes a callous to form over their once Spirit-sensitive conscience.

What if someone who is a teetotaler happens to join the group or eat at the same restaurant? My friend, whom I spoke of earlier, approached me after watching another minister "slam" a few drinks at a wedding reception. Andy had been attending our church for several months and to my knowledge had never heard me teach on this issue or knew where I sat on it, yet he was "blown away" by what he saw at the wedding reception. I doubt the drinking minister intended to abuse alcohol or be the source of confusion, but his insensitivity to those around him led to an unintended stumbling block.

There are so many questions that cannot be answered regarding the stumbling block issue. Why risk it? The only sure way not to be a stumbling block in regards to alcohol use is to not drink. That's why I asked my Romanian brother if in any way our drinking the toast could be a problem. I was unsure whether or not an innocent toast could be a stumbling block in their culture. We drank the toast only after he assured me that it would not be a hindrance to anyone's faith journey.

The fact is: We are our brother's keeper! And whether or not it is wrong in my eyes isn't the point. I must consider his eyes, his perception, his faith journey.

If, in any way, I discourage his walk with Christ, I have done a great disservice to the kingdom of God. And for what? So I can have a glass of wine with my meal? Bring me a Dr Pepper, please!

By the way, the same can be true for a number of other areas of life. I have a fondness for classic rock-and-roll. When I was a youth, all rock-and-roll carried a "sin" label. As an adult, I began to realize that Beethoven wasn't any more Christian than Lynard Skynard and that in careful moderation I could enjoy listening to the music of my youth. So on occasion, Skynard, McCartney, or Frampton can be heard blaring from my office.

As I was leaving the office one day, my secretary asked me if I had been listening to rock-and-roll. "Yes," I answered, "does that surprise you?" She told me it did surprise her. I explained I enjoyed classic rock-and-roll (in moderation of course), and I also enjoyed listening to contemporary Christian music. I explained I liked some of the old rock stuff because it sounded good and brought back good memories of my youth.

Then she said this: "Well, I don't feel like I can listen to rock-and-roll anymore." She told me that it reminded her of what her life had been like before Christ brought so many wonderful changes to her family. She said, "I don't want to have anything to do with my former way of life, if I don't have to." I was sobered and quietly left the office that day, thinking it through again and again. This principle of not causing my brother or sister to stumble kept ringing in my spiritual ears, so I decided to no longer listen to classic rock in my office.

About two weeks went by when my secretary stopped me and asked, "Have you stopped listening to the rock stuff?" "Yes," I answered. When she asked why, I told her that I was wrong in being insensitive to her faith journey and that the very person who led her to faith in Jesus was unknowingly being a stumbling block. She told me that she understood it was different for me and that I didn't need to stop listening to the music. I told her that I had failed to think of her, that the music wasn't nearly as important to me as her walk with Christ, and that I would listen only to that, which was more edifying!

Now obviously this principle has some limitations. There are some Christians who seemingly stumble over every lifestyle choice that differs from their own. Some stumble over believers who subscribe to premium movie channels or regularly attend movies. There are some who believe it is wrong for a Christian to own a luxury car, send their kids to public schools, spend time at the beach, or own a time-share up in the mountains. It's hard to live a somewhat normal life and not be a stumbling block to someone. To the extremist, I will use caution but probably not alter my lifestyle in significant ways. However, there are areas of life that an average, not-so-extreme believer could stumble over, especially if he or she is new to the faith.

My friend Andy is not one of those extremists, nor is he new to the faith. However, it was clear the drinking minister was a potential stumbling block. I don't drink because I don't want to become a stumbling block to other Christians.

Reason number three is especially relevant when befriending or discipling new believers who have been rescued from alcohol and drug dependency. They are recovering from an evil that was sure to put them in an early grave. Most recovering addicts fully understand that they will always be an addict. My lifestyle choices can encourage them or discourage them. When a social-drinking (small-group) Bible study teacher invites the group to his home for a party and alcohol is served, even in moderation, those who are recovering addicts *will* perceive a mixed message, and they *will* likely stumble over a very slippery stone.

We have a men's Bible study in our church, which is made up primarily of recovering alcoholics and drug addicts. Some in the group are veteran followers of Jesus Christ, others are rookies in the faith, and yet, there are usually a couple of not-yet believers in the mix. Each of these men is well acquainted with alcohol. They are not naive to our culture's fascination with fermented drink. They know that not all who drink socially are subject to the same power of addiction that they have struggled to break free from. Yet the issue of Christians who drink socially has "long been a point of confusion," said Jeff, one of the leaders of the study. He explained that almost everyone in the group had come to a tragic conclusion that "nothing good ever comes from intoxication." And even though they recognize that many can drink without it leading to intoxication, they still wonder why risk it. Jeff also made an interesting observation about church leaders. "Church leaders who have the freedom to drink play an even larger role in the potential stumbling of a recovering alcoholic. They either don't understand or don't think it through that one man's freedom can lead to another man's captivity."

For the most part, those who have been through AA will have been taught to refrain from making judgments on another man's drinking. The role of AA isn't to stamp out drinking but to help the alcoholic. But the cold reality is that when a person is recovering from an addiction to alcohol, there is no room for social drinking in their path to freedom, and a spouse or friend or spiritual leader can be a hindrance or a help to the alcoholic by choosing to drink or not to drink.

Not every person will stumble over another person's choice to drink socially. But there are those who will. Some of them will not just stumble; they will fall. The resulting setback could be devastating! Jeff reminded me that this is true of other forms of addiction as well. He said that he has absolutely no compulsion to gamble, but one of the reasons he won't go to a casino or a gambling boat is the potential problem it might pose for the person who has a gambling addiction and looks up to Jeff as a mentor or source of spiritual guidance.

As a person who takes the Great Commission (Matthew 28:18–20) seriously, I must also take serious my lifestyle choices and consider those whom God has graciously placed under my spiritual guidance. Christians, young in their faith, have big targets on their back, and the evil one will use anything he can to discourage them. We are our brothers' keepers, and we must guard not just what we drink but how we work, the words that come out of our mouths, the way we act and react to adverse circumstances, and a host of other lifestyle choices. I don't drink not because alcohol is sinful but because I don't want to become a stumbling block to other Christians.

Barriers

REASON # 4:

I Do Not Drink Because I Do Not Want to Place a Barrier in the Path of Those Seeking God

But among you there must not be even a hint of sexual immorality, or of any kind of impurity, or of greed, because these are improper for God's holy people.

Ephesians 5:3 (NIV)

But you are a chosen people, a royal priesthood, a holy nation, a people belonging to God, that you may declare the praises of him who called you out of darkness into his wonderful light.

1 Peter 2:9 (NIV)

Reason number four will probably create an objection to some since by outward appearance there may not be many non-Christians who would object to any person drinking socially. Many, if not most, yet-to-be Christ-followers do not view casual or social drinking by Christians as wrong. Alcohol consumption is so prevalent in our society that in most parts of our country, it is doubtful that a non-Christian would see social drinking as a barrier or hindrance to their faith journey. But let's stop and examine this point more closely.

One of the problems in our culture is that in recent years there seems to be less difference between followers of Christ and nonfollowers. Many modern (and post-modern) Christian lifestyles are, sad to say, often no different than the lifestyles of nonbelievers. The "salt," as it were, has been losing its "saltiness." Christian distinctiveness is missing in the pews and pulpits of our churches. I'm not talking about wearing out-of-date hairstyles or bland, unattractive clothing or tossing our televisions and computers out of our lives.

Often the only difference between Christians and non-Christians is that one goes to church more often than the other. And even that is becoming less distinctive!

We understand that it's not the keeping of external rules that form the template for true followers, but the fact remains that inner-man's commitments should result in changes to outer-man's lifestyles. I am convinced that not-yet-believing people in our culture are watching those who call themselves Christians. They're inspecting our lifestyles to see if we are relevant yet different from anyone else.

I remember reading of President George W. Bush's spiritual journey to becoming a Christian. President Bush told of coming to a life-changing faith in Jesus after spending personal time with Dr. Billy Graham. He remarked that Dr. Graham had something he admired and wanted. There was something special to Dr. Graham's life—his words, his presence. "He was like a magnet," said President Bush.

That, my friend, is what being salt and light is all about! Something about the man produced a magnetic pull to want to know more. I'm convinced that the not-yet-believing person is desperately hungry to know this kind of person. I'm also convinced that they will seek out his or her God when they get a clear glimpse of the divine as he is incarnate through the life and lifestyle of the average Joe living out an above average life!

As a close friend of mine is fond of saying, we're under constant surveillance. The world is looking for those who are similar yet different. They notice a high road when it's taken, even if they don't totally understand where the road leads or for what reason it's there.

Now I have had a few people tell me they would drink with their lost friends so they could better relate to them and, in fact, build a better bridge for the gospel. (I even had one young Christian leader claim his cigarette smoking was for reasons of outreach and evangelism since he ministered to street people.)

Sounds reasonable. So I have asked everyone who has told me that they drink socially to build a better bridge for the message of Christ one simple question: Did it work? Did you lead your friend to Christ?

To the person, every one of them replied not yet. I've even asked the same question to the same person months later (just in case it took longer than expected), and I hear the same response: "Not yet."

Now you may be different. You may be one of the few who have led your happy-hour friends to faith in Christ. But you are in the minority. I have known more than a few who claim to drink socially to better relate to and thus better evangelize their not-yet-believing friends, yet it doesn't appear to be an effective strategy!

These "happy-hour evangelists" will say things like Jesus loved to party with the spiritually sick because it was the sick who needed the physician. They're convinced that Jesus didn't just attend the parties, he must have partied with them. In other words, Jesus fully participated with and in the nonbeliever's world. Why else would they refer to him as "friend of tax collectors and sinners" (Matthew 11:19 NIV). But the same verse also tells us that Jesus was referred to as a "glutton and drunkard." Now think about that. Do they really think that Jesus was in fact a glutton and a drunkard? Do you? Would Jesus get drunk with his not-yet-believing friends? Would he participate in gluttony? Proverbs 23:2 instructs, "Put a knife to your throat if you are given to gluttony" (NIV). Ephesians 5:18 says, "Do not get drunk on wine, which leads to debauchery. Instead, be filled with the Spirit" (NIV).

Was Jesus overlooking the teaching of his own inspired words in order to evangelize? Or was it that the self-righteous, religious leaders had so separated themselves from the real world that anyone who dared venture into the domain of the irreligious was labeled a sinner too? Was it not the compassion of Jesus for the spiritually "sick" that motivated him to become an authentic friend of sinners? And that he knew he would have to relate to them on their turf rather than his, if he was to gain a listening ear and an open heart? He taught in the temple, but were tax collectors and sinners safe to hear and to inquire there? No. Were they welcome there? Not really. Does spending an evening at a tax collectors party, where wine and food were abundant, mean that Jesus was a glutton and a drunkard too? Not hardly. I do not believe for a moment that Jesus was guilty of violating the very Scripture he inspired, which clearly speaks out against such activities.

Did Jesus drink a glass of wine with them? We know he shared a cup of the "fruit of the vine" with his disciples at the Last Supper on the night he was betrayed. We know he turned the water into wine at the wedding in Cana. I think it is safe to assume that Jesus most likely drank wine in keeping with the custom of the day. However, before you head out the door to stock your liquor cabinet, we must understand there was a considerable difference between the custom of Jesus's day regarding *oinos,* or "fruit of the vine (wine)," and today's. I'll address the issue of wine in Jesus's day more specifically in chapters to follow.

Back to the happy-hour evangelist, I find that their reasoning is faulty! I do not believe it will help bring a person to Christ if you have a beer with them. Unlike the first century when there was little to choose from in regards to safe beverages to drink, we have plenty to choose from today. So I ask for a Dr Pepper.

I've discovered time and again that my ordering a Dr Pepper while my nonbelieving friend orders a beer does not offend him, nor does it prevent or diminish meaningful dialogue. My nonbelieving friends don't think I'm weird because I don't have a beer, nor do they feel like I'm looking down on them if they drink. In fact, they usually think nothing of it.

I have several friends who drink socially, we've been together many times over the course of months and even years both publicly and privately, and they continue to order their drink of choice and so do I. We have wonderful, in-depth conversations about many things, including the claims of Christ and man's need to turn to him for the forgiveness of sin. I have never, *never* felt a need to order a beer in order to be taken seriously. Time and again, new nonbelieving friends will offer me a drink, to which I politely decline and then ask for the Pepper. As our friendship grows, I often perceive a growing interest in my lifestyle choices, which are similar to theirs, yet in some ways different.

Hopefully, our lifestyle choices will raise an appropriate question in their mind. It's not "Why is this guy so strange that he won't drink?" Rather, it should be "What is it about this guy that I find intriguing?" Obviously, alcohol isn't the only lifestyle choice that may be different. I don't use foul language. I don't talk about women in the same manner as they might. I don't tell the same jokes, and I don't use demeaning or offensive clichés in referring to people. To be sure, not all nonbelievers act in these ways either, but the

Christ-follower should have a completeness or whole-ness to their life, which produces a compelling interest from others. In other words, every aspect of our life-style should honor Christ. I believe a man or woman with that kind of lifestyle, lived out in love rather than pride, will create a desire within the minds of their nonbelieving friends to know more.

Now understand something:

> **Being a teetotaler isn't the focus of my faith, but being a social drinker could be a factor in blurring the primary focus of living out a holy life before a holy God.**

Admittedly, there are many Christians, even pas-tors and other Christian leaders, who do not see social drinking as a barrier to their witness. Doubtless, there are social-drinking pastors and Christian leaders who have seen God bless their church and ministry. My caution to Christian leaders is this: Be careful not to confuse attracting a crowd with being an anointed catalyst for radical life change, which is brought about by a person's willingness to submit to the Lordship of Christ. If a pastor or Christian leader finds a crowd willing to follow yet few who have evidence of radical life change, one might question whether or not there is something about his or her teaching or lifestyle that isn't calling others to a radical faith. Remember, the same Jesus who was a friend of sinners also called all who would truly follow him to deny self and to take up their cross.

I find it interesting that studies show that evangelism (or conversion growth) is much higher in more theologically conservative churches. I believe research will also prove that social drinking is less acceptable, especially among the leaders, in more theologically conservative churches. Is there a correlation?

There are signs of explosive growth among some of the emerging churches, which tailor their ministries to reach young adults. Some (certainly not all) of these emerging churches seem to go light on traditional disciplines of the faith, and some may even promote the approval of social drinking. While I rejoice that they seem to be reaching an age group that is missing from many churches, there are serious concerns about the long-term effect of teaching and discipleship that seems to foster a certain disregard for lifestyle practices so closely aligned to a pagan world.

As for now, I still believe the world is looking for light, which will shine brightly in darkness, and salt, which will not only flavor but preserve life. I do not drink because I think it provides a better witness. I believe the choice to have a Dr Pepper over a beer, over the long haul, will help prevent a barrier from forming in the path of those seeking Christ.

The High Road

REASON # 5:

I Do Not Drink Because I Want to "Take the High Road" on a Social Issue

Then the LORD said to Aaron, "You and your sons are not to drink wine or other fermented drink whenever you go into the Tent of Meeting ... "

Leviticus 10:8–9 (NIV)

You must distinguish between the holy and the common, between the unclean and the clean, and you must teach the Israelites all the decrees.

Leviticus 10:10–11 (NIV)

Do you not know that your body is a temple of the Holy Spirit, who is in you, whom you have received from God? You are not your own; you were bought at a price. Therefore honor God with your body.

1 Corinthians 6:19–20 (NIV)

For the kingdom of God is not a matter of eating and drinking, but of righteousness, peace and joy in the Holy Spirit, because anyone who serves Christ in this way is pleasing to God and approved by men. Let us therefore make every effort to do what leads to peace and to mutual edification.

Romans 14:17–19 (NIV)

For he will be great in the sight of the Lord. He is never to take wine or other fermented drink, and he will be filled with the Holy Spirit even from birth.

Luke 1:15 (NIV)

The principle of the high road is that a person may discipline himself or herself as a way to assist his or her devotion or consecration to the Lord. It may help a person maintain spiritual focus and feed a hunger for knowing Christ in a more intimate way. As will be discussed later, it is *not* something intended to set yourself above others or to create an appearance of godliness that will serve only to feed pride and ego. This is between you and God, much like fasting or maintaining a devotional life. This is you making decisions that will ultimately assist in your being set apart to and for God. Would it be a sin to not practice certain spiritual disciplines? No.

***A high road commitment
isn't between right and
wrong; it's the difference
between good and best!***

The verses in Leviticus and Luke refer to a special spiritual commitment *requiring* abstinence from alcohol. What do we take from this? Are these merely exceptional situations? Many will view them as such. Or can we see a principle developing? I believe we can see a principle developing, which I call The High Road Principle.

God set aside Aaron and his sons to be priests and servants. They were to lead and assist others in the practices of worship and sacrifice. You might say they were set apart to serve God in a special way, which required a special commitment. They were to exemplify what it meant to live a holy life wholly consecrated to the Lord. Among other means of commitment, the priests were to abstain from alcohol whenever they served or went into the tent of meeting. Leviticus 10:9 clearly spells out that Aaron and his sons were to "not drink wine or other fermented drink whenever you go into the Tent of Meeting, or you will die." There were practical reasons for this; for example, they needed full use of their faculties in discharging their priestly duties. Leviticus 10:10 explains that a part of their duty was to "distinguish between the holy and the common, between the unclean and the clean." Again, pragmatically, it makes sense that the priests would need a clear head in judging matters of holiness. Any hint of mental impairment could result not only in poor judgment but open the door for sin.

But could it also be a part of God's purpose that the priests were to exemplify a higher calling, a certain "set-apartness" that would result in a demonstration of God-honoring holiness! Commentator J.A. Macdonald has this to say regarding Leviticus 10:8–11:

> The priest needed a clear head, that he might save his soul alive, and that he might fittingly typify Christ… Therefore he must abstain from wine and strong drinks. If sobriety was necessary in the teachers of the Law, it is surely no less necessary in those who teach the vital truths of the gospel… Ministers of the New Testament may become Nazarite if they please; they should at least be Nazarites when holding forth the Word of life.[9]

The idea that they "typify Christ" is what I mean when I refer to their demonstrating a God-honoring holiness. This is what I refer to as the *high road*. It's not that wine would be wrong or sinful in ordinary daily activities, but in the holy service to a holy God, there was a higher calling, a higher road to travel.

The same kind of high road commitment is reported of John the Baptist (see Luke 1:15) and the Nazarite vow (see Numbers 6:1–4). According to the *International Standard Bible Encyclopedia*, a *Nazarite* was one who "consecrated himself or herself, and took a vow of separation and self-imposed discipline for the purpose of some special service, and the fact of the vow was indicated by special signs of abstinence."[10]

Among other things, like being forbidden to cut one's hair during the time of the vow, wine and fermented drink were forbidden! Why abstain from wine? According to the late Bible teacher J. Vernon McGee, "Wine, in the Scriptures, is a symbol of earthly joy; it is to cheer the heart. The whole point here is that the Nazarite was to find his joy in the Lord."[11] Again, this kind of consecration qualifies as a high road commitment.

When it comes to the New Testament church, we see God establishing a set of standards for church leadership. These standards are to promote and place in positions of leadership a person of high road character. In 1 Timothy 3 an overseer is to be "not given to drunkenness." At least that's how the New International Version translates *me paroinon;* the Greek text says, "*me*" (no) "*paroinon*" (beside or alongside wine.)

Most modern translations translate *me paroinon* as "drunkenness" (NIV), "not be a heavy drinker or violent" (NLT), "not a drunkard" (NRSV and NET), or "not addicted to wine or pugnacious" (NASB). Many of the commentators I've researched refer to this as not lingering over wine too long, not being attached to wine or drink, not overindulging in wine, not being unruly and insolent due to wine, or anything else.

It's easy to see why commentators ascribe a qualifier of amount or degree of wine use to *me paroinon,* since wine was such a common drink in the first century and water safe enough to drink was in limited supply. I'll talk more about this in chapter eight, but suffice it to say for now, a certain amount of cultural understanding was applied in both translation and commentary. In this instance it's not necessarily wrong to translate with an understanding of first century culture. But our culture is very different from theirs, and if we take away the amount or degree, we are left with simply the words that God inspired, which are *me paroinon.*

Paroinon combines two words into one: *para,* which means "beside or alongside," and *oinos,* which is "wine." In the original language, it literally means that an overseer (and later, the deacon) was to not be "beside wine."[12] I don't think this refers to physical location, but rather it simply means that the church leader may have a high road to take when it comes to alcohol. Neither in the word or the context is there is a qualifier for the amount of alcohol. It's a simple statement: don't be "with or alongside wine."

The KJV and NKJV actually come the closest to the most accurate translation with "not given to wine." Taken this way, the charge for church leaders isn't a rule to not break but rather a practice to not establish as an ongoing lifestyle. I don't think Paul's intent was to make having a drink of wine a sin for church leaders. Remember, Paul instructed Timothy to take some wine for his stomach problem, which would lead us to conclude Tim had been a teetotaler. It appears that Paul's goal for church leaders wasn't a rule or command but a principled pattern for a lifestyle "above reproach."

There's another word in 1 Timothy that is often missed in the debate of whether or not church leadership should allow or abstain from alcohol in lifestyle choices. First Timothy 3:2 (NIV) says the elder is to be "temperate." In modern English, *temperate* means "to exercise moderation and self-restraint." Consequently, it is taken to mean that the elder is to be free from extremes. One would naturally assume that means social drinking, if properly moderated, is warranted. But that isn't what the word means in the original language.

In the original language the word is *nephalion* and means "not mixed with wine."[13] The classic *Strongs Exhaustive Concordance* informs us that the root word to *nephalion* is *nepho* and provides this as the first option of its definition: "to abstain from wine."[14] Another classic dictionary of New Testament words is that of W.E. Vine, who translates the word *nepho* as "to be free from the influence of intoxicants."[15]

In the least we can conclude that, since wine was a common drink in the first century, Paul may not have meant total abstinence for church leaders, but it can be clearly seen that the behavior and character traits often associated with even the slightest misuse of alcohol had to be closely guarded. A leader that didn't have this area of his life fully under control or in restraint could not be an overseer or deacon.

But let's take it a step further; what if Paul was intending exactly what he wrote, plain and simple? Could it be that the leaders of the early church were to avoid alcohol much like the priests and Nazarites of the Old Testament? Since wine was a common drink, Paul wasn't intending a "don't-touch" stance (remember, he had been a Pharisee and fought against any form of legalism) but rather a "don't-make-a-practice-of-use" stance. It stands to reason that the same high road commitment required of priests and Nazarites in the Old Testament would be the standard for church leadership in the New Testament. The issue of church leaders taking the high road by abstaining from alcohol appears to be both logical and biblical.

Throughout history, God has called certain individuals to a high road of distinguishing "between the holy and the common." Would it then seem biblical, logical, and appropriate for any follower of Christ who wants to devote more of himself or herself to the Lord to voluntarily place themselves under a discipline of devotion or consecration so as to develop and maintain a more intimate walk with Christ? Again, historically, have we not witnessed many who have taken a high road in the disciplines of prayer, scripture memory, Bible study, the regular practice of fasting, or the discipline of solitude? Do we not learn to walk more intimately with God when we pray like E.M. Bounds or exhibit a total-reliance faith like J. Hudson Taylor, who would only ask God and not others for support? Do we not learn the value of scripture memory and a disciplined quiet time when we imitate Dawson Trotman? Does not the evangelistic fervor of D.L. Moody or Billy Graham teach us to walk with Christ in making a lifestyle practice out of sharing our faith with others? Is this not "iron sharpening iron"? (Proverbs 27:17 NIV).

The high road is filled with many means of consecration. It isn't a sanctimonious highway of rules and regulations but a pathway of opportunities to set ourselves apart from mediocrity and a rather common way of living to an uncommon devotion. Abstaining from a lifestyle of alcohol use is just one of many ways that high road commitments can be made.

A warning for those who find themselves on the high road: The high road is *never* to be viewed as a pathway of spiritual superiority. In fact, to treat it as such would undermine the very purpose for taking the road. The proud are never found on the high road. This was one of the key problems of the Pharisees and other religious leaders in Jesus's day. They thought they were taking the spiritual high road with their fasting, tithing, and extreme commitment to ceremonial purity, but their pride prevented God's blessing. I can't help but believe that in their beginning, some 145 years before Christ, the Pharisees were birthed out of pure motives and a passion for God, but somewhere along the line, they lost their first love. By the time Jesus arrived on the scene, their spiritual disciplines were no more than a show room for their self-proclaimed piety. They were in Jesus's words: hypocrites! And their spiritual pride was the target of our Savior's strongest rebuke!

There are those who abstain from any form of alcohol, and they are "darn proud of it!" These people often make condescending remarks about those who drink. They may speak unkindly or critically toward those who don't view this issue in the same light as they do. It is easy for this kind of person to sit in judgment on those who differ. Their "spirituality" actually becomes a stumbling block to other Christians. And their pride becomes a barrier to those seeking the truth of Christ. If you have chosen not to drink and you feel that you are above or better than other Christians who do on occasion have a glass of wine with their meal, then throw this book away right now. You have missed the point! Then pick up a Bible and read every verse you can on pride and humility. The high road is never to be a place to showcase spirituality.

*__The purpose of the high road
is to establish and live out a
standard beyond mediocrity, not
to set yourself above others.__*

It is a process of discovering and choosing that which is better and even best over that which is merely good. The high road is a longing to reach for the prize of the high calling rather than settling for that which is convenient. It is of another world, a kingdom where the values are a cut above. And it is a place of extreme humility. One never truly takes the high road without being covered by the grace and mercy of Christ.

Again, history is replete with examples of individuals who sensed God wanting something more from their lives in demonstration of devotion and commitment. Not all of these examples are worthy of replication; however, some do indeed mark a special commitment and passion for holiness that begs to be imitated.

Alcohol isn't the only common social issue needing the high road treatment. The same can be said of time spent watching television, diet, or exercise. One isn't necessarily sinful for being overweight, but isn't that a rather common road, to take the easy road; and wouldn't the body and testimony be better served if a person took proper care of his body? Get the idea?

I once heard a definition of giving glory to God as "making God look good." Obviously God is good and doesn't need our help to be made to "look" good, but our lifestyles will either reveal his goodness or hide it. I find that there are a few things in life, such as the use of slang or curse words, certain movies, and, yes, even social drinking, that if given up for God with a proper motive and spirit of humility can indeed serve to promote him to a world that wonders if he is a good God! Does this mean that those who choose to drink don't bring glory to God? Not necessarily, but their drinking may ever so slightly blur the lines between the common and the holy, which may shade or hide ever so slightly the goodness of God.

I believe Paul was revealing keys to high road living in 1 Corinthians 9.

> Everyone who competes in the games goes into strict training. They do it to get a crown that will not last; but we do it to get a crown that will last forever. Therefore I do not run like a man running aimlessly; I do not fight like a man beating the air. No, I beat my body and make it my slave so that after I have preached to others, I myself will not be disqualified for the prize.
>
> 1 Corinthians 9:25–27 (NIV)

By living a life of devotion and discipline, I am placing my body into "strict training," which will bring about better focus and even minimize the opportunities to end up being disqualified!

The issue of the high road can encompass many areas of the Christian lifestyle. It can effectively honor God as well as promote him to a world that is all too often stuck in the slow lane of the low road. I have chosen to take what I consider to be a high road on the issue of social drinking for the glory of God, not mine own.

Life-Wreckers

REASON # 6:

I Do Not Drink Because I Do Not Want to Promote One of Our Society's Most Serious Life-Wreckers!

Have nothing to do with the fruitless deeds of darkness, but rather expose them.

Ephesians 5:11 (NIV)

Men of perverse heart shall be far from me; I will have nothing to do with evil.

Psalms 101:4 (NIV)

Do the study. Statistics are overwhelming in regard to the ill effects of alcohol in our society. Is there any substance more linked to societal problems?

Alcohol is the third leading cause of preventable death in the United States and the third leading cause of healthy years lost to death and disability in developed nations."[16]

Some Quick Stats:

- Alcohol is the number one drug problem in America.

- Forty-three percent of Americans have been exposed to alcoholism in their families.

- Four out of ten criminal offenders report alcohol as a factor in violence.

- Three out of four victims of spousal abuse reported alcohol use by the offender.

- Up to forty percent of all industrial fatalities are linked to alcohol consumption/ alcoholism.

- Up to forty-seven percent of industrial injuries are linked to alcohol consumption/ alcoholism.

- Every thirty minutes someone is killed in an alcohol-related traffic accident.

- Americans spend over $90 *billion* dollars on alcohol each year.

- Each year *students* spend $5.5 *billion* on alcohol (more than they spend on soft drinks, tea, milk, juice, coffee, or books combined).

- A typical young person views more than 1,000 commercials for beer, wine coolers, and several thousand fictional drinking incidents on TV each year.[17]

The foundation of a healthy society or community is the family, and alcohol has a devastating effect on families. Family problems that are likely to coexist with alcohol problems include violence, marital conflict, infidelity, jealousy, economic insecurity, divorce, and fetal alcohol effects.[18] Who doesn't know a family that's been divided, broken, or severely traumatized by a family member's alcohol use/abuse? Research has shown that almost one-fourth of Americans (twenty-one percent) experienced at least one alcohol-related problem in the prior year, and approximately one in three Americans engage in risky drinking patterns.[19]

Even though much is being done to discourage drinking and driving, there are still thousands, no make that tens of thousands of people killed each year where alcohol was present in an auto accident. In 2004, for example, 42,636 people died in alcohol-related traffic fatalities, and "an estimated 248,000 people injured in crashes where police reported that alcohol was present."[20] That's an average of one person injured due to alcohol-related traffic accidents every two minutes![21] If that's not sobering enough, get this: "In 2004, 21 percent of the children age fourteen and younger who were killed in motor vehicle crashes were killed in alcohol-related crashes."[22] And you don't have to be in an automobile to be in danger of an alcohol-related traffic crash: "Almost half (forty-seven percent) of traffic crashes that resulted in pedestrian fatalities in 2004, alcohol was involved in either the driver or the pedestrian."[23]

Underage drinking poses many harmful consequences and risks for the individual, their families, and society. "Underage alcohol use is more likely to kill young people than all illegal drugs combined."[24] Dangers associated with drinking and driving have already been pointed out, yet the rate of fatal crashes where alcohol is a factor for drivers sixteen through twenty years old is more than twice the rate of drivers twenty-one and older.[25]

That being said, there are yet other dangers associated with underage drinking. Suicide, sexual assault (including rape), and high-risk sex (having multiple partners and failing to use condoms) are all escalated when combined with alcohol.[26] Stop for a moment and think of the impact that each of these has on a person, their family, their friends, their school, and their future relationships. Alcohol amplifies and multiplies grave dangers for our children. And the dangers don't stop there.

"Exposing the brain to alcohol during [adolescence] may interrupt key processes of brain development, possibly leading to mild cognitive impairment as well as to further escalation of drinking."[27] In fact, drinking during the formative years of adolescence has been proven to increase the likelihood of alcoholism. "People who begin drinking before age 15 are four times more likely to develop alcohol dependence at some time in their lives compared with those who have their first drink at age 20 or older."[28] Drinking during adolescent years of brain development may also "lead to lifelong impairments in brain function, particularly as it relates to memory, motor skills, and coordination."[29]

Alcohol plays a major role in child abuse, assault, manslaughter/homicide, robberies, and burglaries. Studies show that alcohol, more so than other illegal drugs, is linked to violent behavior.[30] Research at the Robert Presley Center for Crime and Justice Studies at the University of California at Riverside found that twenty-five percent (one quarter) of violent assailants were under the influence of alcohol compared to less than ten percent who were under the influence of drugs like heroin, cocaine, or PCP. In cases of homicide, alcohol is "overwhelmingly" the drug most frequently linked to the crime.[31] Robert Nash Parker, lead investigator for the study and professor of sociology, remarks, "If you really want to have effective policies related to drugs, if you want to have fewer bad outcomes in terms of health, welfare, and violence, the drug you want to focus on is alcohol. The evidence is pretty powerful and pretty convincing if someone is willing to look at it."[32]

Parker's words keep ringing in my ears: *If someone is willing to look at it.* I'm reminded of "The Emperor's New Clothes," the Danish fairy tale by Hans Christian Anderson. Do you remember the story of how a couple of swindlers convince the emperor that they have made him a new suit of clothes out of the most beautiful cloth, but the cloth is invisible to fools. Out of fear for their own social status and economic position, the people of the city compliment the emperor's new clothes. They proclaimed that the clothing was beautiful and splendid. Who wants to be labeled a fool? Who wants to lose their job? If it were not for the honesty of a small child who cried out, "He has nothing on," the charade would have continued. I often feel the same way regarding our culture's love affair with alcohol and fascination with drunkenness. Parker is right: We're not willing to look at it. And the sad part is we're being swindled as the charade continues.

The pain associated with alcohol-related consequences is simply beyond measure. How do you put a price tag on broken homes, fractured lives, and terminally damaged relationships? However, the economic cost to our society for alcohol abuse and alcoholism can be measured, and it is staggering. "The financial burden from alcohol abuse and alcoholism on our nation is estimated at $185 *billion* annually."[33] Although those who drink and their families pick up some of the tab, the "nonabusing population also bear costs, such as those related to alcohol-related motor vehicle crashes, crime, and increased health care expenses."[34]

The point simply *cannot* be disputed:

Our society seriously suffers from the use and abuse of alcohol!

From illness to accidents to violence, to self-destructive behavior, to a staggering economic drain on our nation, alcohol seems to be at or near the center of many (dare we say most) of our society's worst problems. I'm not recommending prohibition (although one might be tempted to consider it). What I am saying is simply this: "Hand *me* a Dr Pepper, please!" If I value my society, does it not make sense as well as satisfy a call from Scripture to avoid even the hint of these "fruitless deeds of darkness?"

The sad irony of this life-wrecker is that the popular media will not report the whole story. A study in the November 2006 *Journal of Studies on Alcohol* reported that although alcohol played a part in thirty-four percent of all traffic accidents, only 12.8% of the TV news stories about the traffic accidents mention alcohol. In the same manner, alcohol played a part in thirty-one percent of murders, yet TV news reports about murders mention the "alcohol link" in only 2.6% of their stories.[35] Is this a case of popular culture's being blind or simply unconcerned about the emperor's lack of clothing? To avoid being labeled a fool, have we chosen to foolishly ignore the truth? Or is it a fear of losing our social and economic status?

As I said earlier, I have several friends who are recovering alcoholics. They cannot have one drink! They are teetotalers because of their addiction and disease. They tell me there's not one thing in life that a drink won't make worse. Many of them bear the painful scars of a life once wrecked by alcohol. So fresh is their pain that they often feel very uncomfortable being around friends who drink. If I have the freedom to drink and alcohol is poison to my recovering friend, then I must rethink the use of that freedom, not simply because it may play a part in a relapse but because it can bring back the horrors of a life wrecked by alcohol.

A few years ago, I attended a wedding reception of a Christian couple. Several recovering alcoholics were there. Even though the bride and groom did not drink alcohol, there was an open bar, and several guests participated. Each of my friends in recovery told me later that they felt uncomfortable being around the open bar and the casualness of the drinking. They've been to the dark side, and they want nothing to do with it again.

Alcohol (as a beverage) serves no redeeming purpose in our society! Better stop and read that one again. *Alcohol (as a beverage) serves no redeeming purpose in our society!* According to the Mayo Clinic: "So far, there's no scientifically proven cause and effect between alcohol use and health benefits."[36] Does that surprise you? For years we've read of studies demonstrating at least a few health benefits for those who drink small to moderate amounts of alcohol; however, recent studies have begun to reveal the limitations of previous studies. For example, all the studies supporting small to moderate alcohol use as a health benefit have been purely "observational," meaning "that they either look back at what's affected the health of a group of people or observe a group over time. Results can be skewed by diet, exercise, or other factors."[37] When variables such as age and previous health issues are considered, there is a significant narrowing of the potential health benefit. Weighing these limited benefits against a wide variety of potential risks, it seems clear that alcohol's risks outweigh the health benefits.

While many drink socially without adverse affects, on the whole, alcohol is a common ingredient in many, if not most, of our society's deepest problems. As such, the canvas upon which we paint our lifestyle choices must widen its scope of scenery to include the community that surrounds our often self-focused existence.

Our society has labeled tobacco use as taboo, and in many ways, it is trying to reduce or to remove smoking from the public arena. I don't have a problem with that, since tobacco use does indeed have a cancerous effect on public and personal health. Besides, for those of us who don't smoke, it can be quite unpleasant physically to breathe someone else's tobacco smoke. Cigarette smoke can lead to headaches and sinus problems for many nonsmokers. And since we all end up paying higher insurance premiums and health care costs due to health issues caused by or exacerbated by tobacco use, I don't find anything wrong with limiting its use in public places. There is nothing redeeming about tobacco use.

Our society is trying to create a taboo of being overweight and out of shape. Type 2 diabetes is out of control and due, in large part, to an epidemic of obesity. We count calories, fat grams, cholesterol, and anything else that is seen to contribute to poor health. I applaud each of these efforts, yet we continue to promote alcohol consumption, even though the negative consequences of alcohol abuse and use outweigh all other social ills combined! What am I saying?

Alcohol is a serious life-wrecker, and the Christian must think seriously about whether or not he or she wishes to support its ever-increasing production and consumption!

Ephesians 5:11 tells us plainly to "have nothing to do with the fruitless deeds of darkness" (NIV). That doesn't mean we can coexist with "fruitless deeds of darkness," if we learn to moderate them. I take Paul's words very literally: "Have nothing [nothing] to do with them."

Some will readily point out that it's not the drinking but the drunkenness that is clearly identifiable as "fruitless deeds of darkness," and it's drunkenness that is involved in the aforementioned problems. Be that as it may, we're still to have "nothing to do with it." If drunkenness is a result of being drunk, then what's being drunk a result of? Drinking! Paul's advice? Have "nothing to do with it."

But people will argue that Jesus (and the Bible, including Paul) do not specifically prohibit drinking wine; therefore, they ask, "How can you interpret Paul's advice to have 'nothing to do with' alcohol?"

The point is this: our culture is so saturated with alcohol that its ill effects are not only well documented, but they are a serious peril to our quality and quantity of life! Would Jesus take the same approach to alcohol consumption in our culture as he did in his? Would he do so with the variety of beverages we have to choose from, which are all safe to drink that in his culture were virtually nonexistent? Another question: was the wine (fruit of the vine) of first-century Palestine the same drink we call *wine* today?

I have chosen not to drink because I do not want to promote one of our society's most serious life-wreckers.

Scripture Says What?

REASON #7:

I Do Not Drink Because I Do Not Want to Misapply Scripture!

And the master of the banquet tasted the water that had been turned into wine ... and said, 'Everyone brings out the choice wine first and then the cheaper wine after the guests have had too much to drink; but you have saved the best till now.

John 2:9–10 (NIV)

And no one pours new wine into old wineskins. If he does, the new wine will burst the skins, the wine will run out and the wineskins will be ruined.

Luke 5:37 (NIV)

Stop drinking only water, and use a little wine because of your stomach and your frequent illnesses.

1 Timothy 5:23 (NIV)

Often the primary argument many Christians use to justify casual or social drinking is based on these verses. People will use the above Scriptures to validate their drinking of alcohol by saying, "Didn't Jesus turn the water into wine?" and "Didn't Jesus drink wine and then pass it on to his disciples at the Last Supper?" Before we jump to conclusions, let's take a more in-depth look at the first-century "fruit of the vine."

In the first century, one word described the beverage commonly known today as grape juice, as well as fermented wine: *oinos*. Since unfermented grape juice was difficult to keep due to the lack of refrigeration and modern packaging, much of the *oinos* may have indeed been fermented. According to the *International Standard Bible Encyclopedia*:

> Unfermented grape juice is a very difficult thing to keep without the aid of modern antiseptic precautions, and its preservation in the warm and not over-cleanly conditions of ancient Palestine was impossible."[38]

That being said, there are many scholars who believe that in first-century Palestine distinctions were made between the "new" wine, sometimes called "sweet" wine, and that which was not new.[39] The idea was that the new wine would not have reached full fermentation. For example, in Matthew 9, Jesus uses an illustration to make a point. The illustration appears to assume a common knowledge of not putting new wine into an old wineskin. Then, as well as today, they would carry beverages and, more specifically wine, in a container made of animal skins. It was customary to put wine into goat skins.

New wine was to be placed in new wineskins because the new wine was still undergoing the process of fermentation. The old wineskins were not as supple and soft as the new wineskin. As the wine continued to ferment, it would release gasses that would break the old wineskins because they could not accommodate the expansion caused by fermentation. Therefore, it was advisable to put new wine into new wineskins. Some scholars (see below) refer to this new wine as little more than grape juice. The older the wine got the stronger it became, making new wine less alcoholic and less intoxicating.

Even though Joel is an Old Testament writer of several hundred years before Christ, reliable commentators (Jamieson, Fausset, and Brown) make this comment concerning Joel 1:5 and its reference to new wine:

> *Wine ... new wine*—"New" or "fresh wine," in Hebrew, is the unfermented, and therefore unintoxicating, sweet juice extracted by pressure from grapes or other fruit, as pomegranates (So 8:2). "Wine" is the produce of the grape alone, and is intoxicating (see on Joel 1:10)."[40]

Adding to our discussion of wine in ancient times was the common practice of mixing wine with water. The common cup of wine in Jesus's day was quite diluted. In a wonderful article written several years ago, Dr. Robert H. Stein describes in detail the vast difference between the wine of the first century and that of today. Stein writes:

> [Wine] as a beverage was always thought of as a mixed drink. The ratio of water might vary, but only barbarians drank it unmixed, and a mixture of wine and water of equal parts was seen as "strong drink" and frowned upon.[41]

Did you get that? Even if the wine had equal parts of water and wine (cutting the alcohol content in half), it would be considered "strong drink" and "frowned upon." Stein points out that in both the Greek as well as the Jewish culture, wine was thought of as a mixed drink. It appears that the common water-to-wine mix was two or three parts to one. That means two or three parts water per one part wine.

> In a most important reference (Pesahim 108b) it stated that the four cups every Jew was to drink during the Passover ritual were to be mixed in a ration of three parts water to one part wine. From this we can conclude with a fair degree of certainty that the fruit of the vine used at the institution of the Lord's Supper was a mixture of three parts water to one part wine.[42]

Randy Shuler

Stein also refers to the dangers of unsafe beverages and the difficulty associated with making water safe to drink. "The safest and easiest method of making the water safe to drink, however, was to mix it with wine. The drinking of wine (i.e. a mixture of water and wine) served therefore as a safety measure, since often the water available was not safe."[43]

Generally, wine today is fourteen percent (or less) alcohol by volume. If we assume that the wine was fully fermented, a bottle of wine (fourteen percent alcohol) containing one part wine and three parts water would reduce the alcohol content to somewhere around 3.5% (less if it was new wine).

What am I saying? I'm saying that much of the common wine of the New Testament was little more than grape juice, especially the new wine. Could one get drunk on it? Yes. It was still intoxicating, but a person would have to drink much more of it.

Again Stein says,

> To consume the amount of alcohol that is in two martinis by drinking wine containing three parts water to one part wine, one would have to drink over twenty-two glasses. In other words, it is possible to become intoxicated from wine mixed with three parts of water, but one's drinking would probably affect the bladder long before it affected the mind.[44]

The water Jesus changed into wine at the wedding in Cana was called "choice" or "good" wine. The Greek word *kalos* means, "better, good, beautiful."[45] "Good" or *kalos* wine was a better tasting, more quality wine. That Jesus produced a wine that was of better quality and taste shouldn't surprise us. Yet there are those who believe this too could be a reference to unfermented wine. Historical authors such as Pliny and Plutarch attest that "good wines" were those which *did not intoxicate*.[46]

There are many unanswered questions regarding the miracle at Cana. Did Jesus turn the water into fully fermented wine? Since it was wine made from water, did Jesus purposely dilute the wine with enough water (as was the custom of the day) to have high quality but low alcohol content? Was the drinking of wine at a wedding in the first century similar to or different from the way alcohol is served at many weddings today? We don't know the exact answers to these questions; however, it would be hard to imagine Jesus adding anything to the wedding festival that would promote drunkenness or altered states of consciousness.

As I said earlier, there were similarities between the first-century alcohol consumption and our twenty-first-century American culture, yet there were also radical differences in the way drunkenness was regarded. Wine or juice from the grape was a normal everyday drink in first-century homes. Drunkenness could be a problem then (as it is today); however, their culture strongly frowned upon drunkenness. They would have come down hard on those who were inebriated. It's doubtful they would have provided establishments (i.e. bars) for the sole purpose of drinking or "loosening up" after work or "getting waxed," because life had just handed them a rotten egg. That would have been taboo in the social climate of the Mideast.

New Testament scholar A.T. Robertson makes this comment regarding the miracle at Cana as found in John 2:9:

> Unlike the Baptist, Jesus mingled in the social life of the time, was even abused for it (Mat 11:19; Luke 7:34). But this fact does not mean that today Jesus would approve the modern liquor trade with its damnable influences. The law of love expounded by Paul in 1 Co 8–10 and in Rom 14; Rom 15 teaches modern Christians to be willing gladly to give up what they see causes so many to stumble into sin."[47]

Another difference between our culture and that of the first century is in the area of humor and entertainment. Our culture finds being drunk humorous. Foster Brooks made a living acting drunk. That in a nutshell appeared to be the sum of his acting skill. It was his gift to American entertainment, and we laugh. For some strange reason, we find it amusing to watch an inebriated person try to carry on a conversation, walk up a flight of stairs, or perform simple tasks. The Internet is stocked with videos and pictures of drunkenness intended for our enjoyment. I have serious doubts that the people of the first century would see Foster Brooks or our fascination with drunkenness as humorous. We make videos of teenagers binging on alcohol during spring break and call it "having a good time." Again, I doubt the Jewish culture of the first century would refer to their "kids gone wild" as "having a good time." I believe they would be ashamed of such indecencies. I believe they would condemn rather than condone this type of annual springtime migration to the warm beaches of Florida and Mexico.

(Note: I recognize not all spring breakers are bent on debauchery and drunkenness. Many take to the beaches, cities, as well as rural areas, to give a hand to those in need or share their time and faith with peers.) I'm not bashing spring break or warm beaches; what I am saying is this:

Our culture is similar to the first century in that alcohol is a part of everyday life but different in the manner in which alcohol is consumed and much different in how drunkenness is tolerated and often promoted.

Even in modern times, Middle Eastern culture continues to view alcohol and drunkenness very differently from our North American culture. *Easton Bible Dictionary* makes this comment:

> Wine is little used now in the East, from the fact that Mohammedans are not allowed to taste it, and very few of other creeds touch it. When it is drunk, water is generally mixed with it, and this was the custom in the days of Christ also. The people indeed are everywhere very sober in hot climates; a drunken person, in fact, is never seen.[48]

If a person tries to make a case for alcohol consumption based on the verses mentioned at the beginning of this chapter, they are really stretching God's word to try to make it fit. People see the word *wine* in the Bible and more specifically in Jesus's ministry and jump to the conclusion that Jesus would approve of their social drinking. They fail to take into consideration the enormous differences between our cultures in both the actual drink and the overall view of drinking it.

In 1 Timothy 5, Paul instructed Timothy to use wine, a "little" wine, for medicinal purposes. Tim was a young pastor in a church, where it seems those older than him were giving him grief. Evidently, Tim was a teetotaler because Paul had to encourage him to drink a little wine for "his stomach" and "frequent illnesses." Oil and wine were often the best medicines available in the first century. The medicinal aspect of alcohol hasn't changed all that much in almost 2000 years. Read the labels on many of our modern medicines, and you'll discover small amounts of alcohol have been added to certain treatments and remedies.

My grandfather was a farmer who kept a bottle of whisky around for one purpose: to give a teaspoon of it to a new calf that was born a little on the weak side (especially in the winter months). He, as well as other farmers, would use this small amount of alcohol as a medicinal elixir to help the newborn calf get a good start in life.

I know what some of you are thinking: *Sure, that's what he wanted you to believe, "It's for the calves."* But I remember as a youth watching the contents of that same bottle change by only a few teaspoons year after year. I also knew anyone who drank from that bottle would be in deep trouble, and because the contents rarely changed, it would be obvious if someone were indeed to take a nip or two. Granddad's bottle was limited to medicinal purposes.

By the way, for those who claim they drink wine for its health benefits, the medical community does in fact tell us that drinking a glass of wine every day or two may stand to improve certain aspects of a person's health. However, as previously stated in chapter seven, it is uncertain the benefits outweigh the risks. What's even more interesting is that the medical community is now discovering we can get similar health benefits by drinking grape juice! And grape juice doesn't have the inherent risks associated with red wine!

In a very interesting article titled "The Buzz about Grape Juice," WebMD reports:

> The latest studies show you can get almost all the same benefits (of wine) from grape juice. The reason: Purple grape juice contains the same powerful disease-fighting antioxidants, called flavonoids, that are believed to give wine many of its heart-friendly benefits. The flavonoids in grape juice, like those in wine, have been shown to prevent the oxidation of so-called bad cholesterol (LDLs, or low-density lipoprotein) that lead to the formation of plaque in artery walls.

In a study published in 1999 in the journal *Circulation*, researchers at the University of Wisconsin Medical School in Madison asked fifteen patients who already showed clinical signs of cardiovascular disease—including plaque-constricted arteries—to drink a tall glass of grape juice daily. After fourteen days, blood tests revealed that LDL oxidation in these patients was significantly reduced, and ultrasound images showed changes in the artery walls, indicating that their blood was flowing more freely.

Grape juice can also lower the risk of developing the blood clots that lead to heart attacks, according to unpublished findings from Georgetown University researcher Jane Freedman, M.D. So can red wine, but in this case grape juice is the more practical way to go: "Wine only prevents blood from clotting (when it's consumed) at levels high enough to declare someone legally drunk," says University of Wisconsin researcher John Folts, Ph.D. "With grape juice, you can drink enough to get the benefit without worrying about becoming intoxicated."[49]

The medical community adds that drinking more than a glass of wine a day turns the positive affect of alcohol into a gross negative.

Once again, the problem with wine is not in the glass of wine itself, it's in the overall social acceptance and promotion of both its use and abuse in our culture. If our culture used wine as they did in the first century, if our culture was to get serious about drunkenness as they were in the first century, and if our culture were to take precautions with the alcohol content so that the glass of wine had minimal intoxicating power as it was in the first century, well, then a Christian in our culture might have grounds for relating his or her social drinking with the aforementioned Scriptures. But since there is a world of difference between our culture and that of the first century, in both the wine and the drinking of it, I find a person hard-pressed to make a case for social drinking based on Scripture.

That doesn't mean that a Christian should feel condemned for having a glass of wine, but it should seriously challenge the thinking that a lifestyle of social drinking is a biblically sanctioned lifestyle practice for the fully devoted believer.

It's Just Not Necessary

REASON #8:

I Do Not Drink Because It Simply Isn't a Necessary Part of My Diet!

How much better to get wisdom than gold, to choose understanding rather than silver!

Proverbs 16:16 (NIV)

admit this argument, at first, appears to be weak. What does personal necessity have to do with it? Before you skip this chapter, read a little further. If you grasp this concept, you may find it useful in many areas of life, not just whether or not we drink alcohol. Let me explain.

In various parts of the world, there simply isn't

much to drink that is clean and healthy. The prevalence of water contamination combined with the lack of available soft drinks and juices provide a sense of need to have an uncontaminated drink, even if it were in some small degree fermented. However, here in the good ole' U.S., life couldn't be more different. Our choice of beverages appears limitless. It is to this fact that reason eight begs the question of why? Why if I have so many beverages to choose from do I choose alcohol over equally tasteful refreshments that do not carry the potential risks of alcohol? I have come to the conclusion:

Some decisions in life are not necessarily wrong; they're just not necessary.

If for no other reason (and as you can tell, I believe there are at least ten reasons to not drink), I still don't see the necessity of drinking alcohol. It's just not a necessary part of my life. Proverbs reminds us it is better to live life with wisdom and understanding than living it for the common goals of our culture (gold and silver).

This concept can apply to several aspects of life and lifestyle. I know several godly Christians who have accumulated a considerable amount of wealth, yet by choice they live below their means in order to be more generous to others and God's kingdom work. They choose a lifestyle devoid of many of the luxuries that money can buy, simply because they just don't see it as a necessary part of their life.

I've admired people who do not live in the most expensive home they can afford or drive the most expensive car they can make payments toward. There is nothing wrong with having money and nothing wrong with enjoying the fruits of hard work; however, isn't frugality a remarkable virtue? Being frugal can liberate a person to be able to bless others in very tangible ways.

Along the same line of thinking, some people have removed television from their lifestyle, while others limit it because they simply don't see it as a necessary part of their life. They fill their time with other activities that they deem more beneficial than merely watching TV. Is it sinful to watch television? Not necessarily, but the use of, as well as the abuse of it, could certainly be an unwise or even foolish use of time.

In the same light, I just don't see alcohol as necessary to my diet or social life. One of the key questions I ask myself is why would I want to have a beer when I could have a Dr Pepper, an orange juice, lemonade, Gatorade, sweet tea, or water? I just don't find it necessary to spend the extra dollars for a beer or glass of wine. It won't enhance my taste buds. It won't add anything to the meal or friendly conversation. It might give me a buzz, and that goes against my moral understanding that I should exercise self-control over my mind and tongue at all times. Alcohol can certainly lessen the ability to control those two important areas of a person's life.

It doesn't take being drunk to be affected by alcohol. An alcohol buzz always leads to mental fuzz! How many times has a man made unwarranted, over-friendly advances toward a woman who was not his wife because he's been a little too relaxed by a couple of beers? I once attended a party where most of the guests were drinking beer or wine. I observed a friend of mine greet another man's wife in a way that caused her to jump back and move away from his uninvited, slightly overfriendly greeting. I know my friend and I don't believe he was intending to startle his guest, nor was he intentionally flirting with her, since she was a longtime friend. Yet it seemed alcohol had loosened healthy inhibitions ever so slightly. Nothing was made of the issue, nor should it have been, but how many times has such an unguarded touch or word led to something that was so unnecessary?

I just don't get it. Why do people feel the need to always be holding an alcoholic drink in social settings? Is it really that it tastes that much better than other drinks? Or is it possible that many drink because it makes them feel fashionable or trendy. There's a certain persona that goes with holding a drink in your hand, ordering a glass of wine by name, or offering a full service bar to friends at a party held in one's home.

I've watched people order an expensive glass of wine with their meal, take only a drink or two from it, and leave the rest in the glass. I want to know why. Why order if you're not drinking it? Why do we do these things? Do we do these things because we're thirsty? Do we do them because we very much like the drink? Or do we do them because they make us look or feel a certain way?

A few years ago, I attended a party where the (Christian) host served virgin drinks to her guests. She went through all the steps to make the drink just like the original except without alcohol. Virgin drinks were being handed out right and left. This too seemed foolish to me. In my mind's eye, the person (and people) appeared to be acting like eight-year-old kids puffing away on candy cigarettes. A certain unspoken "coolness" is pursued, and to me, it appears silly when grown adults, especially those presumably maturing in the Lord, behave in such a shallow manner.

I just don't see the necessity of drinking an alcoholic beverage, if you have as many options as we have! A more important question in my mind is why don't all restaurants serve Dr Pepper? They certainly seem to stock a wide assortment of beer and wine!

I recognize that one can develop a taste for alcohol, and people like the way it tastes—eventually. Yet I think my experience with alcohol is overwhelmingly common, that a taste for beer and even wine takes some acquiring. If that's true, then why do we put ourselves through the paces to acquire the taste unless we feel the cultural pressure to drink? That brings us to the ninth reason I don't drink socially.

The Moldy Mold

REASON #9:

I Do Not Drink Because I Want to Guard Against Being Squeezed into the World's Mold

Do not conform any longer to the pattern of this world, but be transformed by the renewing of your mind. Then you will be able to test and approve what God's will is—his good, pleasing and perfect will.

Romans 12:2 (NIV)

Then he said to them all: "If anyone would come after me, he must deny himself and take up his cross daily and follow me."

Luke 9:23 (NIV)

Our society doesn't just accept alcohol; it pushes it! No, it presses it into our psyche to the point we think we can't have a pizza without a cold draft. We can't have a good time with the buddies unless we have a Bud Light in our hand. We can't eat at a formal restaurant without a glass of merlot, and we can't have a party unless there's a full bar of beverages to offer.

Weddings, as well as wakes, flow with alcohol. Ballgames, as well as ballroom black-tie events, are saturated with the stuff. Advertisers spend over two billion dollars annually (that's $2,000,000,000) on it, and American consumers spend $90 billion a year drinking the stuff.

The Christian community fought against this sort of thing for a long time. But in recent years, we've not just given up the fight; many have joined the other side.

Christ-Follower, we are not to *follow* the way the world thinks! If the world thinks that drinking is totally normal or acceptable, then red flags should be waving. The world tends *not* to get things right! They may be wrong with this one as well! Where is the Christian community in light of our culture's fascination with alcohol? If the salt loses its saltiness, it is "no longer good for anything" (Matthew 5:13 NIV).

Is there a connection between the Christian community's shift toward adopting the culture's thinking about alcohol (and other social issues) and the decline of evangelistic efforts?

Is evangelism more difficult today than in years past? Is church attendance and involvement less than it was fifty years ago? Is there a decline in traditional moral values and beliefs?

Obviously, alcohol alone isn't to be blamed for these and other post-modern trends away from God. However, acquiescing to and ultimately selling out long-held convictions regarding lifestyle choices, which include social drinking, is a part of the process of being squeezed into a mold that's become ever so moldy! It's high time to rethink the issue. Paul teaches us in the twelfth chapter of Romans that transformational living starts with transformational thinking!

A *renewed* mind is key to transformational thinking. One of the works of the Holy Spirit is to take the inspired truth of Scripture and transform us from the inside out by reshaping the way we think. The Spirit renews not only our thoughts but also the process of how we think and why we think what we think!

A renewed mind doesn't settle for compliance to mere rules of living but strives to understand the basis for God's laws and principles. God's laws and principles are not for his benefit but for our benefit. Yes, every command is meant to make life better for us, not worse. Since God made us and knows exactly how we best function and since his desire is for us to function, humanly speaking, at peak performance (i.e. life full and meaningful, see John 10:10), he has provided us with an owner's manual complete with instructions, examples, and case studies to teach us not only how to live life but why we're to live the way of his call.

Jesus began to separate the truly interested from the merely fascinated by teaching in parables. Often, at the close of one of his sessions of instruction, he would say, "He who has ears to hear, let him hear." I'm sure there are many ways to interpret this little phrase, but to me it's like saying, "Stop a minute and think this through. Don't miss what I'm saying!"

Think, Christ-Follower, think!

A dangerous shift has and is currently taking place within the church in America. There has been a growing accommodation to the culture among American evangelicals. On the whole and in a general sense, American Christianity has relaxed its standards on many fronts.

Christian colleges have lightened up on once firmly held guidelines. For example, many now have co-ed dorms where thirty years ago it wouldn't be a consideration. Movies that used to be taboo are now commonplace for Christians. A movie containing a nude scene would have been opposed by the Christian community of thirty years ago. Today, it almost goes without notice. We simply overlook that which Hollywood "must do" to sell a movie in order to participate with our culture. My parents would not let us watch *Laugh-In* because Goldie Hawn danced around in a bikini. Television today makes Goldie appear as though she were a Puritan. (That's a scary thought, isn't it?)

I'm not advocating a return to an era of Victorianism, where prudishness and repression seemed to be high marks of the society. What I am saying is that as a Christian culture, we are well on our way down the slippery slope of moral relativism and compromised discipleship. What is the cost of following Christ these days? Is there a cost in America? What do Christians say no to these days? What are the things that Christ-followers deem off-limits in our culture?

I've been amazed—no—I've been shocked at some of the things I see Christian leaders deem appropriate for lifestyle practices. Alcohol use isn't the only issue, although it always seems to be not far away. Let me ask you, reader, would you consider hot-tubbing with friends where the wives go topless as an appropriate behavior for Christians? What if the Christian is a pastor of a church? Let's don't kid ourselves into thinking that the issue of alcohol is "much-to-do-about-nothing." The dots between alcohol use among believers and other questionable lifestyle practices do connect!

Regarding our American culture, this can be expected. The Bible reminds us that the devil is the ruler of this earth. Ephesians 2:1–3 boldly proclaims that:

> You were dead in your transgressions and sins, in which you used to live when you followed the ways of this world and of the ruler of the kingdom of the air, the spirit who is now at work in those who are disobedient. All of us also lived among them at one time, gratifying the cravings of our sinful nature and following its desires and thoughts. Like the rest, we were by nature objects of wrath. (NIV)

These are great insights about the world we live in, yet a disturbing question is raised in my mind:

In today's American Christianity, modern, and even more so among post-modern Christians, is there a "past tense" to our current lifestyles?

How many Christians can truly say, we *were* dead in sins or we *used* to live like that at one time?

The things we're willing to watch, the places we're willing to go, and the words we're willing to use, as well as the beverages we're willing to drink, are they not surprisingly similar to the rest of our culture? Is there any wonder that the passions of our hearts, as well as the issues of integrity, seem to align quite comfortably with the rest of our culture? Do most Christians demonstrate a life-changing encounter with the living Lord where lifestyles, as well as souls, have undergone a transformation? Or has there been any measurable change at all?

Granted, there have been advances in the kingdom work that were long overdue and needed. The use of newer and various translations of the Bible, as well as newer forms of worship and creative ways of communicating the gospel both inside and outside the walls of the church, have been great for the church. Casual dress, worship at times other than Sunday morning and in places other than the church facility, use of technology, and new means to engage our culture are positive steps forward for the church in an emerging, post-modern culture. I'm on board with living out a missional faith! But does missional faith necessitate cultural liberality?

There are areas where the Christian community has or is, in my opinion, in danger of being or going out of bounds. In fact, in some areas of this new, emerging Christianity there seems to be a severe stretching of the limits of Christian freedom!

I recently read an article about a very popular post-modern Christian author who was praising another "Christian" author because she could drop the "F-word" into her writings and get by with it. My question is simply this: why would this be a good thing? Suddenly, it's chic to be a Christian and freely use the F-word? Pagans have been using it for years, and outside of Hollywood and hip hop, it's never been chic!

I think—we have stopped thinking. Renewed thinking has been replaced by renewed feeling. "I feel it is okay for me to drink. I don't feel bad about it, so it must be fine with God." This "feeling" our way to behavior is a serious yet subtle shift in the way Christians make decisions and develop habits of lifestyle. Obedience, however, according to God's word, never depends on whether or not we feel like following the command. Obedience, by definition, means to obey, whether we feel like it or not.

In the Old Testament, God forbade the children of Israel from marrying foreigners. In Nehemiah we read that God loved King Solomon and made him king over all Israel. We read that among the nations there was no king like him. Yet, according to Nehemiah, Solomon, the wisest man in the world and blessed of God like none other, was led into sins because he married foreign women. What followed was disastrous for both Solomon and the kingdom!

It would appear that the church in America has been courting our culture for years, and now we're on the verge of joining our hearts and souls in marriage to not just a foreign but to a fallen bride. Some would say we've already done this, and, in many ways, I am inclined to agree.

In light of being squeezed into the world's (moldy) way of thinking, alcohol is just one mistress among many! The ninth reason I choose not to drink is because I want to guard against being squeezed into the world's mold. The tenth reason for *not* drinking alcohol socially concerns the future generation and those we love the most. It also may be the most important of the ten reasons I choose not to drink.

My Kids

REASON #10:

I Do Not Drink Because I Want to Help My Children Develop Clear and Consistent Beliefs and Practices Regarding the Use of Alcohol

The righteous man leads a blameless life; blessed are his children after him.

Proverbs 20:7 (NIV)

Deliver me and rescue me from the hands of foreigners whose mouths are full of lies, whose right hands are deceitful. Then our sons in their youth will be like well-nurtured plants, and our daughters will be like pillars carved to adorn a palace.

Psalm 144:11–12 (NIV)

've seldom seen a home where social drinking was acceptable to the parents that the kids didn't encounter problems with alcohol. Sad to say, in our society it's difficult to find any home, Christian or non-Christian, alcohol present or absent, where the children haven't encountered problems with alcohol. Yet it has been my experience in twenty plus years of ministry, in families where social drinking is acceptable for the parents, the children have a more difficult time with the abuses of alcohol. I don't have statistics on this, just observances, and these observances cut across all evangelical denominations.

It also needs to be said that just because a family abstains from social drinking that there is *no* guarantee the children won't struggle with alcohol. But the odds of reducing such struggles are in favor of the teetotaler, especially when it comes to parents who are willing and unafraid to address alcohol problems and issues with their children.

I've counseled numerous parents who were experiencing serious problems with their teenager's underage drinking. When the parents' own lifestyle includes social drinking, I'm often left wondering how you can tell your children not to drink when they so readily observe alcohol use in the home by the people they trust the most. It sends a mixed message!

I know what many of you are thinking, *Drinking in moderation isn't condoning drunkenness!* And I agree with this statement based solely on its own merits. However, in the context of raising a family, especially teenagers, the desired intention of this statement seldom hits the mark. Let me explain.

Let's assume the parent has their alcohol consumption moderately under control, no drunkenness, just an occasional social drink. Yet they can't figure out why their children go to a party and get wasted or why their children go away to college, and suddenly, there's a drinking problem. They don't understand how their precious daughters can go on spring break and saturate themselves with so much alcohol that they lose what seems to be all restraints, disrobing to the amusement of all onlookers. "That's not the way we raised our children!" the bewildered parent cries. And still the parent fails to connect the dots!

Here's an important lesson to learn about teenagers:

Whatever an adult does moderately, the teenager will do excessively.

Music, sexuality, recreation, or alcohol—it doesn't matter. Listen to the way they talk. Extreme, isn't it: "I might as well die," "That sucks," and "She's an idiot."

That's one of the reasons teenagers are not considered adults. They have not yet learned self-control. The best way to help them is for parents to use a greater amount of self-control in their own lives. When a parent speaks of moderation, the teenager hears "Go for it!" When you consider just how deadly alcohol can be if abused by extreme behavior, one has to seriously wonder why even have it in the house?

I listened to the shock of one particular parent when they discovered that their "locked" liquor cabinet had been raided. Much to the parents' surprise, they discovered that the vodka bottle had been refilled with water, not vodka. I wonder how much of that fifth of Vodka the child (or his friend) drank and in what amount of time. As little as six to eight 1.5 ounce glasses of hard alcohol drunk within an hour can lead to fatal alcohol poisoning. Would the parent leave a loaded gun in a glass cabinet shielded by the flimsiest of locks tempting their inquisitive teenager to impress his or her friend? Probably not! And if the parent found out that their child had broken into the cabinet and had played with the loaded gun, would the parent seriously consider selling the gun or getting it out of the house? Likely. The deadly affects of alcohol poisoning cannot be overstated.

I don't know why, but I'm still amazed at the occasional senselessness of intelligent people! One parent informed me that they had purchased alcohol for their underage teenagers in order for them to have a party at their home based on the reasoning, "They're going to do it anyway; at least they won't be driving." A father of a Yale-bound student told me he not only bought the alcohol for his son and four of his buddies but also rented a hotel room to throw their party based on the same reasoning, "At least they're not drinking and driving."

Did this parent set a guard over the room to keep others away? What happens when the girls show up? What about date rape? Binge drinking? Alcohol poisoning? Future addiction? Moral character? And, oh yeah, it's *illegal!*

An AMA poll of teens released in August of 2005 discovered that one in four had attended a party where minors were drinking in front of parents.[50]

Here is the reasoning of some short-sighted parents: By having alcohol in the home and by demonstrating moderation, they take away the novelty of alcohol, and their teen won't be so likely to go wild at college or on spring break!

While there may be a sliver of truth to the idea that a teen can be overprotected from the issues of the world, the reverse reasoning of having alcohol in the home to reduce the likelihood of alcohol abuse isn't logical. If it were, then it would also stand to reason that if I demonstrate adultery (in moderation of course) to my children, they will be less infatuated with sexual immorality and actually remain sexually pure. Hogwash. Life doesn't work that way. That which is demonstrated as moderately acceptable by adults will be pursued to the extreme by teens. Why? Because that's the nature of teenagers.

If we tell our teenagers to "not drink; however, since we know you will, it's okay to drink if you do so in our home," we send a message that's both confusing and conflicting. Tracy Toomey, epidemiologist at the University of Minnesota's School of Public health, says when "We say, 'Don't drink alcohol.' Then we say, 'But it's okay to drink in this situation.' Such mixed messages may actually make it more likely that kids will drink when parents aren't around."[51]

We must come to grips with some sobering facts about our children's abuse of alcohol. Dr. J. Edward

Hill, president of the American Medical Association, says:

> The perception out there is that 90 percent of teens get alcohol using fake IDs and by going to bars. That's not true. They are getting it from social sources: parents, older friends, older siblings and others. Parents need to become aware of the fact that a large percentage of alcohol comes from their own homes or the homes of other parents.[52]

In an April 2005 Teenage Research Unlimited survey, sixty-seven percent of teenagers responded that it was easy to get alcohol from their own home without their parents' knowledge. Forty percent report ease in getting alcohol from someone else's parents while thirty-six percent get alcohol from their parents *with* their parents' knowledge.[53]

Again, Dr. Hill says,

> Parents may not understand the toll of underage drinking. Research shows underage drinking plays a large part in teen crime, violence, sexual activity and accidents. Underage drinking can lead to addiction or other substance abuse, affect school performance and damage the developing brain. A child who begins to drink before the legal drinking age may end up having a significant problem with reasoning and memory because of alcohol use. That kid is not going to do as well in school. Parents are not as aware (of the consequences) as they should be.[54]

As parents of four children, three post-college and one in college, my wife and I have been affirmed time and again in multiple ways that it has been a right choice not to include alcohol in our home and lifestyle.

To the parents of the "overprotected" child: If you have chosen an alcohol-free lifestyle, you would do well to talk with your children about alcohol and why you have chosen not to drink! Don't mark it simply as taboo or evil. Talk about it in ways that make sense. Start early in the child's life to carefully point out the fallacy of advertisement and the lure of the world wanting to make a dollar as well as the evil one wanting to make a mess of families. There also must be a consistent demonstration of compassion for those who differ. This is precisely where Jesus shined. He was a friend of sinners, not an enemy. If a judgmental attitude toward those who drink is perceived by your child and they eventually discover that those you're sitting in judgment on don't sit in judgment on you, you run a real risk that your child will abandon your principles to follow others who demonstrate a kinder, more loving spirit.

The bottom line to the tenth reason is that my children stand a better chance of developing a clear and consistent belief and practice regarding alcohol if I choose not to drink.

Some children readily accept their parents' pattern of moral beliefs. "Mom and Dad don't drink alcohol; they say it's not necessary, so I won't drink either." These compliant children will have a clear principle of life to follow. No mixed message here. The boundaries are clearly drawn, they're satisfied to stay within the boundaries of the people they know and trust the most, and that produces security!

Other stronger willed children often seem bent on learning life's lessons the hard way. These headstrong, independent children will have to try it themselves. When they begin to experience the ills of alcohol (throwing up, hangover, feelings of guilt, acting in shameful ways, etc.), they will know firsthand why their parents have chosen not to drink. Hopefully they will begin connecting the dots for themselves. If they are raised in a home where social drinking is a lifestyle, some of the essential dots are missing.

In a national survey (Uhlich Report Card 2004), teens from across the country say that their parents often fail to "lead by example when it comes to drug use." Parents earned a grade of *C-* from teens who were asked how they thought parents were doing in stopping underage drinking. Sheryl Brisett-Chapman, executive director of the National Center for Children, says "teens consistently tell her that adults do a poor job of leading by example with their own behavior."[55]

Listen, our children live in a world full of mixed messages. They hear one thing at church and another at school. They see one thing at home and another at the movies. They read one thing in the Bible and another on MySpace or Facebook. As parents, we must be diligent about sending a wholesome, unmixed message to our kids. Our message should be a message where faith, lifestyle, and social interaction have virtue and consistency.

Life lessons, including alcohol use, are learned individually; however, parents must set the example! In light of my experience, children develop a clearer and more consistent belief and practice regarding alcohol if their parents have chosen not to drink.

A Caution to Teetotalers

For those of us who have made a decision to *not* include alcoholic beverage as a lifestyle practice, how do we interact with others, especially other believers, who see nothing wrong with it? The apostle Paul has some strong yet insightful words from his letter to the Colossians to guide us.

> Therefore do not let anyone judge you by what you eat or drink, or with regard to a religious festival, a New Moon celebration or a Sabbath day. Colossians 2:16 (NIV)

Being forgiven and set free by Christ, Paul warns us to not let anyone condemn us for what we eat or drink. One would safely assume that he also intends that neither should we condemn nor judge each other for what they eat or drink. Paul's admonition comes on the heels of those who had come to Colosse teaching the new Christians the necessity of keeping certain holy days and festivals as well as distinguishing between clean and unclean meat and drink. It seems he also might have been confronting a pre-Gnostic heresy of extreme asceticism being mixed into the faith disciplines of Christianity. As often happens with legalistic religion, judgmentalism, pride, and spiritual elitism were disrupting the beauty of being in a loving relationship with Christ. It was robbing Christians of the joy and freedom they had found in Christ (Colossians 2:9 NIV). Legalism had become a catalyst for division within the body of Christ. Wherever pride and judgmentalism reside, there will be disunity!

Specifically, Colossians chapter two addresses these errant issues of trying to gain or maintain a relationship with God by keeping certain rules of religious observance as well as rigidly observing what to eat and drink and what not to eat and drink. In other words, the heresy was the belief that one's righteousness was dependent on rule keeping. This teaching was wrong in both practice and theology, as only a relationship with Christ is the key to being right with God. Paul spells out with clarity that the reality of true religious practice is found in Christ. Christ had fulfilled the Old Testament sacrificial system. As Paul would say to the Galatians: "It is for freedom that Christ has set us free" (Galatians 5:1 NIV).

So to be clear, the passage in Colossians does *not* specifically (or intentionally) address the issue of the spiritual acceptability of a social practice, such as drinking a glass of wine at a meal. This passage addresses a ceremonial (legalistic) approach to faith and how ceremony and ritual can never satisfy what only a relationship with Christ can provide.

That being said, I do find a warning in this passage to those who choose to abstain from certain food or drink. Whether vegan or a teetotaler—in the very least—there is a warning in Colossians that we must not overlook!

We must be careful how we relate to others in the body of Christ, or we might find ourselves guilty of wrongly judging or condemning one of our brothers or sisters in the faith.

We can voice our preference. Even explain, dialogue, and teach what God has led us to conclude about social drinking. We can encourage, exhort, and certainly exemplify our lifestyle choice of abstaining from alcohol consumption. But we must avoid condemning those who disagree with us!

Since food and drink are not essential to gaining or maintaining a relationship with God, it is advisable to resist making it an issue of divisiveness between brothers and sisters in the kingdom of God.

This is easier said than done! How many families have been ravaged by alcohol abuse where the door to such pain was left open by a tolerant lifestyle? It is most difficult not to throw all social drinkers in the same basket as we see the social evils of alcohol bludgeoning our neighborhoods and family reunions.

Yet to "insist on self-denial" (Colossians 2:18 NLT) would place us in the company of first-century Judaizers, imposing rules in order to gain a right relationship with God, or in the company of the pre-Gnostic teachers, perpetuating the false ideals that the physical body and pleasure were evil.

As we relate to fellow Christians, we must use caution not to turn a very good idea and lifestyle practice into an equation for holiness. Holiness, if we're not careful, can be relegated to a form of self-orchestrated piety. Throughout Christian history, there have been people who viewed holiness simply as an adherence to strict and rigid disciplines.

> ***There is no power in discipline and devotion if it does not stem from a pure heart and humble attitude.***

There is a very real danger of appearing to be holy without actually being holy. We must not allow abstinence from alcohol to become an issue that might cheapen holiness. In other words, we run the risk of cheapening holiness, if we who don't drink view ourselves more spiritual or closer to God than those who have an occasional glass of wine with their meal.

Abstinence from alcohol must stem from a heart already clean and set apart to God. To communicate, intentionally or unintentionally, that avoiding alcohol is a way to be more holy or to gain a closer access to God could lead us to a path well traveled by the likes of Judaizers, Gnostics, and Pharisees.

Actually, we will have a much larger audience and impact if we exemplify our lifestyle in a nonjudgmental fashion. Then when asked why we don't drink, we must be ready to give a clear answer. In most social settings, you won't have an opportunity to go through all ten reasons, so don't force it! That would be tantamount to preaching, and your friend isn't asking for a sermon. If you respond with just enough but not too much, then you will likely have another chance to explain more later. At that point, be ready to articulate even more clearly your lifestyle preference and what led you to this decision!

Avoid clichés and pithy responses that might put up a barrier rather than build a bridge to your friend. In the same light, never act ashamed of your decision or that you "can't" drink, as though God won't let you. What good will it do to have a lifestyle practice, such as abstaining from social drinking, if at the same time you communicate it's something you really want to do, but God won't let you. If you're attempting to honor God with a lifestyle choice but your attitude and mind-set fall short of sincerely honoring him, you miss the point. Jesus told people who were fasting to wash their faces and comb their hair so as not to draw the wrong kind of attention or self-admiration.

Over the years, I have been surprised at how many people notice and become interested in my choice to not drink. I have been amazed at how many people consider this a big issue, yet there seems to be little thought given to sound reasons not to drink (and even less written on the subject to help a person come to a more complete understanding of the issue). The popular culture is obviously going the other direction, and it's taking much of the Christian culture with it. I find this disheartening. Yet I also believe that in the years ahead, more and more Christians will come to a redefining of their position toward alcohol. Sadly, many will come to their decision to not drink only after suffering through the pain of alcohol abuse of either themselves or someone very close to them.

That being said, Christian, you must think this issue through and be able to articulate clearly a more thorough understanding of reasons not to socially drink. And when you do, you must absolutely do so without condemning fellow believers.

A Caution to the Emerging Christian

Earlier I referred to some churches experiencing numerical growth (some of them, rapid growth), especially among young twenty- to thirty-year-olds. Many of these churches identify themselves as a part of a movement to more effectively live out the faith in a post-modern culture. They are often referred to as emerging churches. I applaud these emerging churches for their nontraditional worship (which sometimes returns to ancient-future), skillful use of multimedia, and use of narrative to communicate the story of Christ. I commend their passion for reaching out to others with the message of Christ. I find their creativity and willingness to think outside of the box refreshing! Their efforts to be missional and incarnational have gripped the hearts and minds of many young (and veteran) Christ-followers. The cultural landscape is changing and in many ways will require the church to adjust its form or style of ministry. How can we more effectively "do church" and, yes, "be church" in the emerging generation, and how are we to meet our culture with the always relevant message of Christ are vital questions to seek to answer.

However, we must use caution so as not to change the message of Christ or his Word. Whether by proclamation or doctrinal formation or practical application, we must remain true to the Scriptures, as they have stood the test of time. I don't think I'm alone in observing some areas of this movement that cause concern.

This is not the time or place to define or compare the distinctions of the emerging, the emergent, or other missional attempts to contextualize the gospel message within our post-modern world. (I recognize the stark differences between "emerging" and "emergent" churches and respective movements.) Even within the emerging church, there is a wide diversity of positions and theologies being sorted out. Again, this is not the place to dissect the emerging movement. My focus is narrow. I also realize it is unfair to lob generalizations into a single phrase such as "emerging"; however, to more clearly identify a potential problem within a particular segment of post-modern evangelicalism, I refer my caution to the "emerging Christian."

I have a concern that long-term commitments to Christ could be forfeited if discipleship and holiness are ignored or compromised within the teaching and training of the emerging church. As stated earlier, not all who identify with the goals and ideals of the emerging movement practice the same behaviors within their church culture. But more than a few do support or exercise behaviors that were once deemed inappropriate for serious followers of Christ. From using profanity in the pulpit to pastoral blogs that are sexually explicit to light-hearted treatment of alcohol consumption, it would appear there is a considerable amount of compromise in lifestyle arenas.

All too often the desire to relate to the post-modern world has taken emerging leaders and their followers to an edgy, even trendy lifestyle that differs little from a culture that is ruled by the prince of darkness. Absent is a discipleship, where discipline is actually employed, and a holiness, where purity is actually pursued. In some situations, traditional forms of discipleship are not only shunned, they're mocked and ridiculed. And holiness seems to have disappeared from the emerging conversation.

As noted in the previous chapter, holiness is much more than rule keeping or simply abstaining from alcohol! Often people have the erroneous idea that holiness means being "more spiritual." To restate it, if a person thinks he or she is "more spiritual" because they don't drink, their self-appointed piety misses the mark. Besides, I'm not sure what "more spiritual" really means. I just know it doesn't mean holiness.

Holiness is a separateness issue where we are still "in" the world but no longer "of" the world. To be holy means to "be set apart" to and for God. It means to be separated *from* sin *to* God. According to W.E. Vine, "*hagiasmos* translated 'holiness' … signifies (a) separation to God, (b) the resultant state, the conduct befitting those so separated."[57]

In 1 Peter 1:15–16, Christians are called to holiness: "But just as he who called you is holy, so be holy in all you do; for it is written: 'Be holy, because I am holy'" (NIV).

The *Broadman Commentary* on this passage says,

> Basically, holiness means to be set apart. God is holy in that he is set apart from all others and from every thought or act which could be called sinful, unrighteous, unjust, etc. He calls his people to be like Him.[58]

This definition of holiness is affirmed in the *Expositors Bible Commentary:*

> The basic idea of holiness in the Bible is that of separation from all that is profane. The developed sense of holiness includes various meanings translated into English as "purify," "sanctify," "separate from," "dedicate," etc.[59]

The reason I go to such lengths regarding holiness is very simple: Holiness is a concept easily misunderstood. It's kind of like a group of people, blind from birth, trying to describe what an elephant looks like by merely reaching out and touching whatever part of the elephant is closest to their outstretched hand. Their descriptions of the elephant would depend solely on what part of the elephant they touched. You have to see the big picture before the pieces of the picture make sense.

Some have taken holiness to simply mean "saying no" to a list of bad things. Holiness is more than rule keeping. Still others mistake holiness as merely an intention of the mind, which has very little effect on tangible lifestyle practices. This too falls short, as it deprives holiness of its "wholeness" aspect. According to the *International Standard Bible Encyclopedia,* "Christ's people are regularly called 'saints'—or holy persons...holiness in the high ethical and spiritual meaning of the word is used to denote the appropriate quality of their life and conduct."[60]

Christians are to live a *set apart* lifestyle because they have been *set apart.* In multiple places in the New Testament, followers of Christ are called and commanded to "put off" the old patterns of the world and "put on" the new patterns of Christ. Should that include lifestyle matters of how we talk (whether or not to use foul or vulgar language in conversation), what we allow our eyes to watch, and what jokes or stories we find amusing, as well as whether or not we choose to drink socially? Shouldn't all these lifestyle matters be brought under the influence of Christ and the teaching of his Word?

To the emerging Christian, please use caution and discernment when following teaching that downplays tangible aspects of personal holiness. If we're not careful, we could be seeing an emerging version of "itchy ears" where people will "not put up with sound doctrine" but to "suit their own desires, they will gather around them a great number of teachers to say what their itching ears want to hear" (2 Timothy 4:3 NIV).

Many will claim that those they are reaching out to cannot be expected to follow the ways of holiness and that they must take the gospel to them rather than expect them to come to the gospel. I couldn't agree more! I support, practice, and teach a missional approach to reaching out to our friends with the love of Christ. I do not expect my not-yet-believing friends to act like followers of Christ. Neither do I expect them to discover Christ by merely coming to church. I take the gospel to them by entering their world, attending their parties, and loving them the way they are. I don't hint at or suggest they change their lifestyle practices other than encouraging them to seek to know Christ in a personal way.

But I do not find it necessary to use the same language, laugh at the same jokes, or even drink the same drink in order to become their friend and to be taken seriously!

What I find interesting is that many of the emerging churches seem to most readily attract the twenty- and thirty-year-olds who are either already Christians or were raised in Christian homes. It seems to me that this age group of Christian young adults fall into one of two camps: in one camp are those carrying on the banner of their parents' faith with like-minded passion and commitment, while in the other camp are the mavericks who have broken from the *lifestyle patterns* of their parents' faith. Notice I said that they have broken with the *lifestyle patterns*, not necessarily the faith. And again, it's just my observation, but it seems that these young adults (who have been raised in church and many have been believers since childhood) are looking for a church where they can worship God and participate in kingdom service without having to give up many of their current lifestyle choices.

On the one hand, I find it encouraging that there are churches who can and do attract these young mavericks; however, on the other hand, I fear that the teaching of God's Word is being sifted to accommodate lifestyles. If this is true, then in the end their faith will be nothing more than a religious fad.

Indicators of this "freedom" to live an emerging faith are not limited to lifestyle choices of whether or not to drink alcohol but a host of other choices as well. Their daily speech seems to have no conscionable objection to using foul or vulgar language. There seems to be no censorship of movies or books, even when they blatantly promote excessive violence, sexual perversity, or a fascination with evil. There also seems to be little thought given to their own sexual purity. Yet they are quick to sit in judgment on their parents' faith. Again, I'm not referring to the not-yet-believer or even a new believer. These are the lifestyle patterns of those who are supposedly serious about God yet disenchanted with their parents' form of faith.

For the time being, it seems to be working, but will there be negative consequences down the road? Will these new seeds of faith emerge into fully devoted followers of Christ who carry the message on to the next generation? Or will they end up being religious fads in the end choked out by the weeds of undisciplined lifestyles? Obviously, that's a question we cannot know the answer to now, but we must be concerned about it now to avoid the potential of problems later. To those in the emerging church, please be careful, and while you're at it, could you get me another Dr Pepper?

Working It Out

As stated at the outset, I have ten reasons not to drink. Each reason is to be considered individually on its own merit, yet they also must be viewed together as a whole.

Any one reason, alone, may not carry enough weight by itself to persuade you to abstain from social or casual drinking. You might debate the applicability of one or two points. However, taken together (within the context of our North American culture), the evidence appears *overwhelming!* For me, a foundation for a lifestyle principle has been laid. This is not simply a rule to *not break;* it is a principle to live by. It isn't that I can't have a glass of wine or even a beer, but the principles formed by Scripture lead me to adopt an attitude that genuinely chooses not to drink. I'd rather have the Dr Pepper. Sure, there may be the rare exception, but as a lifestyle practice, I choose not to drink alcohol. In the Christian walk, there will likely be several lifestyle choices that are made with the intent to either honor God, to prevent barriers to the gospel from being built, or to protect other believers from being tripped up on their faith journey. The choices I have made regarding social drinking are based on three things: Scripture, experience, and sound reasoning.

I have friends who view alcohol use differently. We're still friends. I don't feel it necessary to preach at them or refuse a dinner appointment because they will have a drink with their meal. I seldom see a glass of alcohol as the culprit. The sin, for me, is *not* in a few ounces of fermented grape juice.

> **The problem comes as I ignore the teaching of Scripture that there may be a better way for me to live!**

There is a better way to lead and influence others, especially those of my own family, than the way of the culture. There is a way to live that, when lived out in a nonjudgmental, humble manner, will profoundly stand apart from the culture. It can even have a powerful effect on the culture.

What would Jesus do in our culture? That's a good question, isn't it? We know what he did in his culture. But in our culture, with the way alcohol is made, promoted, and abused today, what would he do? I'm sure he would spend quality time with people who were in need of what only he can provide. I'm quite confident he would meet people on their turf. He would go to their parties without a list of dos and don'ts. He would make people feel genuinely loved. And he would be authentic, true, and real. But what would be his choice of drink? In our culture? Would he ask for a Bud Light, or would he opt for one of the many less-fermented options? You can call me crazy, but I think if he had the choice, we just might hear him say, "Hand me a Dr Pepper!"

Epilogue

Late one night last summer, I received a phone call that a former member of our church was being life-flighted to a local hospital with serious injuries. The family of six had been active members of our church, until they had to move out of state. They were a good family! Dad and mom worked hard and were fully engaged in the lives of their four kids. They loved the Lord and had been in the center of activities at church and school. Since we no longer had weekly contact with them, the message on the phone came with a certain surprise and urgency. The injuries must be life-threatening or, in the least, very serious to life-flight their son, a junior in high school, to a hospital in St. Louis.

Our student pastor and I reached the hospital even before the life-flight arrived, and we learned through phone conversations that the father had died in the accident. Dad had been driving a motorcycle with his son sitting behind him when he lost control of the bike. They left the road and smashed into a tree, taking Dad's life and leaving his son with some serious injuries.

The medical team at the hospital soon discovered that the son's injuries were not as life-threatening as they expected, even though he was severely bruised and banged up. He did have a concussion and began telling us (once we were allowed to see him) that he should have stopped his father. In almost a whisper, he was saying, "Dad was drunk." Family members thought the concussion or trauma was having an ill effect on the son, as Dad wasn't a drinker. Later we learned it was true.

Evidently, Dad had secretly begun to have more than just an occasional drink. The family didn't know about his private progression with alcohol. They were shocked that he might have been drunk on the night of the accident. Close friends were shocked. No one knew. At first, no one would believe it. From time to time, he would drink a beer, but not enough to be considered even a social drinker. Why did he do this? What was he thinking? He had been such a good father. He had been such a good husband. He was a good man! He loved the Lord. He loved his family. He was fun-loving and easygoing. He spent a lot of time camping, hunting, and fishing with his family. Yet for whatever reason, he was inebriated the night he pulled his son onto the back of his motorcycle, and it cost him his life. It cost Debbie her husband. It also cost his kids their dad.

This is a sad story. And it was so unnecessary.

A few months after the accident, I had an opportunity to sit down and talk with Debbie and her children. I explained that their dad was a good dad and that nothing he did that fateful evening should take away or diminish their admiration for their father. He had been a good man! But neither should they ignore the fact that he made a bad decision that night, a decision involving alcohol that cost him his life and them their father.

How many times does this happen across our nation? Whether it's a father or a son or a daughter or a friend, this is not an uncommon tragedy. The potential for danger is always there, isn't it? Do you see why Solomon, the wisest man in the world, writes: "Do not gaze at wine when it is red, when it sparkles in the cup, when it goes down smoothly! In the end it bites like a snake and poisons like a viper" (Proverbs 23:31–32 NIV). Not all snakes are poisonous, and not all snake bites end in death. But the question remains; why play with snakes at all? Why risk it?

In our culture, with as many outstanding beverage options as we have, I just don't get it. Why do we need a beer? Why do we need a drink? As my good friend Jeff, who leads the Bible study for guys in recovery, recently told me, "God has given us a billion things to enjoy in this life. Why would someone be so arrogant to think that they need a billion and one?"

Debbie and her family are coping. They're healing. Family, friends, church, and the Lord are all helping hold this family together and move them on in life. But if we can help prevent other families from having to go through what Debbie and her family have gone through, maybe one father's death, tragic as it is, won't be a total loss. All I'm saying, dear friend, is that we must really think through this issue. The problem, as stated in the beginning, isn't in that glass of wine or beer in and of itself. I'm not proposing rules of don't touch or don't taste or don't handle. This has more to do with lifestyle patterns than an occasional glass of wine. What I am saying is that once you consider the whole of Scripture and understand the realities of the many negative effects of alcohol on our culture and our Christian witness, I find a compelling argument to simply abstain. So I invite you to join me at the bar as I order another round of—Dr Pepper!

Bibliography

APPEARANCES

1   "Romans-Revelation," *Clark's Commentary on the Bible*, vol.6, Adam Clark, (New York, Nashville, Abingdon-Cokesbury) p 555.

A POTENTIAL PROBLEM

2   National Institute on Alcohol Abuse and Alcoholism, "A Family History of Alcoholism: Are You at Risk?" pub no. 03–5340, Aug 2005.

3   National Institute on Alcohol Abuse and Alcoholism, "A Resource Guide," <www.niaaa.nih.gov> April 2005.

4   National Institute on Alcohol Abuse and Alcoholism, "Alcohol Alert—No. 60," <http://pubs.niaaa.nih.gov/publications/aa60.htm> July 2003.

5   National Institute on Alcohol Abuse and Alcoholism, A Family History of Alcoholism: "Are You at Risk?" pub no. 03–5340, Aug 2005.

6   National Institute on Alcohol Abuse and Alcoholism, "The Collaborative Study on the Genetics of Alcoholism: An Update," <http://pubs.niaaa.nih.gov/publications/arh26–3/214–218.htm>June 2003.

7   American Heart Association, "Alcohol, Wine, and Cardiovascular Disease," <www.americanheart.org/presenter.jhtml?identifier=4422>>

8   Mayo Clinic Staff, "Alcohol and your health: Weighing the pros and cons," <www.mayoclinic.com/health/alcohol/SC00024> Aug 25, 2006

9   "Leviticus 10:8–11," *The Pulpit Commentary,* Volume 2, Leviticus-Numbers, J.a.m., Spence and Exell ed., (Wm. B. Eerdmans Publishing Company, 1950) p 163–164.

10 Orr and Nuelson, *International Standard Bible Encyclopedia,* (Hendrickson pub 1994.)

11 J. Vernon McGee, *Thru the Bible: Volume 1,* (Thomas Nelson, 1990.)

12 Frank E. Gaebelein ed., *The Expositor's Bible Commentary:* Volume 11, (Zondervan, 1978) p 364.

13 Ibid, p 364.

14 James Strong, *The Exhaustive Concordance of the Bible,* (Holman Bible Publisher) Number 3525 in "Greek Dictionary of the New Testament."

15 W.E. Vine, *Vine's Expository Dictionary of Old and New Testament Words,* (Revell, 1981, Volume 4) p 44 under the word "sober."

16 National Institute on Alcohol Abuse and Alcoholism, "A Resource Guide," <www. niaaa.nih.gov> April 2005.

17 *Alcohol Statistics,* Narconon of Southern California, <http://www.drug-statistics. com/alcohol.htm> 2007.

18 National Institute on Alcohol Abuse and Alcoholism, "Alcohol Problems in Intimate Relationships: Identification and Intervention," <http://pubs.nih.gov/publication/niaaa-guide/index.htm>.

19 Ibid.

20 National Center for Statistics and Analysis, "Public Traffic Safety Facts," 2004 <www.nhtsa.dot.gov>.

21 Ibid.

22 Ibid.

23 Ibid.

24 National Institute on Alcohol Abuse and Alcoholism, "Underage Drinking: A Major Public Health Challenge—Alcohol Alert No. 59," April 2003.

25 Ibid.

26 Ibid.

27 Ibid.

28 National Institute on Alcohol Abuse and Alcoholism, "Young Adults Drinking—Alcohol Alert No. 68," April 2006.

29 Ibid.

30 "Alcohol More Strongly Linked to Violence than Other Drugs," *Join Together,* <www.jointogether.org/news/research/summaries/2002/alcohol-more-strongly-linked.html>- Jan 28, 2002.

31 Ibid.

32 Ibid.

33 National Institute on Alcohol Abuse and Alcoholism, "A Resource Guide," <www.niaaa.nih.gov> April 2005.

34 National Institute on Alcohol Abuse and Alcoholism, "Health Services Research—Alcohol Alert No. 69," July 2006.

35 "Media Violence Reports Rarely Mention Alcohol," *Join Together*, <www.jointogether.org/news/research/summaries/2006/media-violence-reports-rarely.html> Oct 25, 2006.[ref.Slater, M.D., Long, M., Ford, V.L. (2006) "Alcohol, Illegal Drugs, Violent Crime, and Traffic-Related and Other Unintended Injuries in the U.S. Local and National News," *Journal of Studies on Alcohol*, 67(6): 904–910.]

36 *Mayo Clinic Health Letter*, "A Drink For Your Health? Not So Fast," Mayo Clinic, November 06, 2003.

37 Ibid.

SCRIPTURE SAYS WHAT?

38 "Wine, Wine Press," *International Standard Bible Encyclopedia*,(Eerdmans 1915)

39 Ibid.

40 "Joel 1:5, *Commentary Critical and Explan-atory on the Whole Bible: The Book of Joel,* Robert Jamieson, A.R. Fausset, A.R. and David Brown, (1871)

41 Robert H. Stein, "Wine-Drinking in New Testament Times," *Christianity Today,* June 20, 1975: 10

42 Ibid.

43 Ibid.

44 Ibid, 11.

45 "John 2:10" *Barnes' Notes on the New Testa-ment,* (Baker, 1983) Albert Barnes.

46 "Number 2570 in Greek Dictionary of the New Testament." *The Exhaustive Concor-dance of the Bible.* James Strong (Holman Bible Publisher)

47 "John 2:9.", *Robertson's Word Pictures of the New Testament* A.T. Robertson (Broad-man Press 1932,33, Renewal 1960)

48 "Wine," *Easton Bible Dictionary*, (Matthew George Easton, 1897)

49 "The Buzz about Grape Juice," *WebMD*, 3 April 2000 http://www.webmd.com/diet/features/buzz-about-grape-juice

MY KIDS

50 Derek Burnett, "Safe at home?" *Readers Digest October* 2005: 139.

51 Ibid, 140.

52 Shari Roan, "When parents buy the booze; Teens don't usually need fake IDs to obtain alcohol, a new study shows, because it's easier to get alcohol from their families or older friends." *Los Angeles Times*, 8 August 2005: F1

53 Ibid.

54 Ibid.

55 Todd Zwillich, review by Brunilda Nazario, MD, "Adults Get Low Grades on Drinking, Drugs," *WebMD Medical News,* 22 June 2004<http://www.webmd.com/ parenting/news/ 20040622/ adults-get-low-grades-drinking-drugs>

A CAUTION TO THE EMERGING CHRISTIAN

56 "Holiness, Holy, Holily."*Vine's Expository Dictionary of Old and New Testament Words,* W.E. Vine (Revell, 1981, Volume 4)

57 Ray Summers, *The Broadman Bible Commentary,* Volume 12, Hebrews - Revelation, (Broadman Press, 1972) p 153.

58 Frank E. Gaebelein ed., *The Expositor's Bible Commentary:* Volume 12,

59 "Holiness" *International Standard Bible Encyclopedia,* (Eerdmans 1915) (Zondervan, 1978) p 224.

listen|imagine|view|experience

AUDIO BOOK DOWNLOAD INCLUDED WITH THIS BOOK!

In your hands you hold a complete digital entertainment package. In addition to the paper version, you receive a free download of the audio version of this book. Simply use the code listed below when visiting our website. Once downloaded to your computer, you can listen to the book through your computer's speakers, burn it to an audio CD or save the file to your portable music device (such as Apple's popular iPod) and listen on the go!

How to get your free audio book digital download:

1. Visit www.tatepublishing.com and click on the e|LIVE logo on the home page.
2. Enter the following coupon code:
    fd8c-0330-c257-7a09-7fca-fb55-ffaf-4ed7
3. Download the audio book from your e|LIVE digital locker and begin enjoying your new digital entertainment package today!